Robert Barnes

A BASIC GRAMMAR
OF THE
GREEK NEW TESTAMENT

BY

SAMUEL A. CARTLEDGE

A.B., A.M., B.D., PH.D.

PROFESSOR OF NEW TESTAMENT

COLUMBIA THEOLOGICAL SEMINARY

DECATUR, GEORGIA

ZONDERVAN PUBLISHING HOUSE

GRAND RAPIDS, MICHIGAN

First Published 1959

PRINTED IN HOLLAND
BY DRUKKERIJ HOLLAND N.V., AMSTERDAM

PREFACE

This basic grammar is written for the specific purpose of helping students read their New Testament in Greek. They may be students in college or seminary, ministers in the field, or intelligent laymen. It is assumed that the student has gone through some beginners' Greek book, in either Classical or *koine* Greek.

An attempt has been made to concentrate on the essentials. There is a place, of course, for the fuller grammars, and it is to be hoped that at least some students who use this grammar may be inspired to go beyond it in the direction of making themselves real scholars in the Greek language; then they will need to master many of the details of the language that are not treated here. But the inclusion of such details in a brief grammar tends to confuse and discourage the large number of students who are not yet, and may never be, ready for them.

The order of presentation of the material has been determined by the needs of the reader of the New Testament. So often grammars seem to be arranged on the basis of the assumption that the student is preparing himself to translate English into Greek; certainly some practice in that is wise in a class for beginners' Greek. But when that is completed, most students have the very utilitarian purpose of reading the Greek of the New Testament so as to learn as accurately as possible its real meaning.

A glance at the table of contents will show how the reader of the Greek New Testament will be able to make easy and ready use of the material in the grammar. The chapter divisions largely follow the parts of speech. When the student is dealing with a word, he must first determine what part of speech it is. Then he can turn to the appropriate chapter and find out what he needs to know in order to find the meaning of the word. Two chapters each are given to nouns and verbs. The first chapter in each case deals with the forms. Paradigms are given that will enable the student to determine the form of virtually every noun or verb used in the New Testament. Then the

5

next chapters will enable him to determine the meaning of his particular form with which he is wrestling, as he deals with the usages of the nouns and verbs. For example, he may spot a noun form as being in the genitive case. But how can he translate it? What does the genitive case mean? He can turn to the treatment of the genitive case where he will find all the usages of that case. Then he can ascertain which of the usages will best fit the context with which he is working.

There is no way to avoid much pure memory work in trying to learn Greek—or any other language. But an attempt has been made to give help in showing the student how certain forms are constructed. In connection with the paradigms, the student is helped to break the form down into its constituent parts. Then he will be able to look for the distinctive signs that will help him identify the various forms. Thus reason can come to the aid of memory. The total task is lightened, and the student can become far more sure of his results than if he had to depend upon his memory alone.

The standard grammatical terminology has been used as much as possible. Every effort is made to keep it as simple as can be and to let the name of the usage suggest the translation as often as possible.

In dealing with noun forms, the five-case system has been used. The author feels strongly that that is both simpler and more logical, since the Greeks developed only five case endings. Those who prefer the eight-case system can adapt the paradigms easily and even the usages without too much difficulty.

The author cannot begin to express his gratitude to those who have been his teachers and those who have written in the field of Greek grammar, both Classical and *koine*. The author is, of course, responsible for any errors that may be in this grammar; if they are called to his attention, an attempt will be made to correct them in future editions.

SAMUEL A. CARTLEDGE

Columbia Theological Seminary
Decatur, Georgia

TABLE OF CONTENTS

Page

CHAPTER I

THE ALPHABET

Capital	Small	Numerical Value	Name	Pronunciation
A	α	1	alpha	a as in father
B	β	2	beta	b as in bed
Γ	γ	3	gamma	g as in get (ng before $\varkappa$, γ, or χ)
$\varDelta$	δ	4	delta	d as in dig
E	ε	5	epsilon	ĕ as in get
Z	ζ	7	zeta	z as in zero (dz within words)
H	η	8	eta	ē as in fete
Θ	ϑ	9	theta	th as in thin
I	ι	10	iota	ĭ as in pin; ī=ee as in feel
K	$\varkappa$	20	kappa	k as in kin
$\varLambda$	λ	30	lambda	l as in look
M	μ	40	mu	m as in man
N	ν	50	nu	n as in new
$\varXi$	ξ	60	xi	x as in fix
O	o	70	omicron	ŏ as in not or as in obey
$\varPi$	π	80	pi	p as in pin
P	ϱ	100	rho	r as in rat
Σ	σ, ς	200	sigma	s as in sin
T	τ	300	tau	t as in top
Y	υ	400	upsilon	u=oo as in fool
$\varPhi$	φ	500	phi	ph as in Philadelphia
X	χ	600	chi	ch as in loch
$\varPsi$	ψ	700	psi	ps as in epsilon
$\varOmega$	ω	800	omega	o as in note

Notes:

1. The Greek numerical system used the letters of the alphabet as the numerals. Three old letters were employed: F, or digamma, for 6; Ϙ, or koppa for 90; and ⅅ, or sampi, for 900.

2. The capital letters are used less frequently than in English. They are used for proper names and for the beginning of paragraphs. Some editors use them to introduce direct quotations.

3. Two forms of small sigma are in use: ς is used when it is the final letter in a word; at other times, σ.

4. There is little uniformity in the pronunciation of omicron; when it is pronounced as in not it is easily confused with alpha, but when it is pronounced as in obey it is similar to omega.

5. Westcott and Hort use the uncial letters for quotations from the Old Testament. They are so much like the capital letters that they can be easily recognized, except that the uncial sigma is C.

6. There is no letter of the alphabet for the English h. The sound is found in the letters ϑ, φ, and χ. At the beginning of a word it is indicated by "breathings." Every Greek word beginning with a vowel must have either a rough breathing, indicating the h sound, or a smooth breathing, indicating that there is no h; e.g., ἁ=ha, or ἀ=a. Every word beginning with a rho has the rough breathing; e.g.. ῥέω. The breathings are placed above the small letters and in front of the capitals (ἀ, ʽA).

7. The letters λ, μ, ν, and ρ are called liquids, because they do not stop the flow of the sound.

8. Nine of the consonants may be arranged in a table thus:

	Labials	Dentals	Gutterals
Hard	π	τ	κ
Medium	β	δ	γ
Aspirated	φ	ϑ	χ

9. Long and short vowels. η and ω are always long. ε and o are always short. a, ι, and v may be either long or short.

10. The pronunciation of diphthongs:

αι = ai as in aisle
ει = a as in fate (some pronounce it as i in fight)
οι = oi as in oil
υι = we
ευ = eu as in feud (or a quick ĕ + oo)
ηυ = a as in fate + oo as in food
αυ = ou as in out
ου = oo as in food

11. Breathings or accents are always placed over the second vowel of a diphthong.

12. Iota subscript. Some Greek forms require the iota subscript, an iota written below an η or an ω (ῃ and ῳ). These iotas are necessary, but they are not to be pronounced.

CHAPTER II

ACCENTS

Accents are always written on Greek words in modern printings of the Greek New Testament. The earliest manuscripts did not have the accents, and the accents of the later manuscripts varied rather widely. Editors and readers are free to change accents whenever they feel that a change will improve the sense. This will not give as much leeway as might at first be thought, as usually only one accent will be right with each word.

Because Greek words have their accents written, it is perfectly plain as to which syllable should receive the stress. There is no excuse for accenting the wrong syllable in reading Greek.

The accent is always written over the vowel in the stressed syllable (over the second vowel of a diphthong).

There are three Greek accents: the acute (á), the grave (à), and the circumflex (â). Originally the different accents seem to have indicated a difference of musical pitch, but now they simply indicate stress and are pronounced alike. In usage, however, the three accents must be kept distinct.

Greek accent works from the last of a word toward the front, so the following terms are often used to designate the syllables: the ultima is the last syllable; the penult, the next to the last; the antepenult, the second from the last. The accent never goes back beyond the antepenult.

In reading from Greek to English, the student does not need to worry too much about the rules of accent. They are of great importance in writing Greek.

GENERAL RULES FOR ACCENT

1. An acute accent may stand on the ultima, penult, or antepenult.

2. A circumflex may stand on an ultima or a penult.

3. A grave may stand only on the ultima.

4. A circumflex may stand only on a long vowel or a diphthong.

5. In a sentence, an acute on the last syllable is automatically changed to a grave unless the word is followed by some mark of punctuation.

6. In a word with a short ultima and a long penult, if the penult has the accent it must be a circumflex.

7. If the ultima is long the accent cannot be on the antepenult.

8. All long vowels and diphthongs are long, but final οι and αι are treated as short for accent purposes.

VERB RULES OF ACCENT

9. Verb forms have recessive accent; that means that the accent is placed as far from the last syllable as the general rules of accent will allow. The few exceptions to this rule can be learned in the paradigms; most of the exceptions are infinitives and participles, which are nouns and adjectives as well as verbs.

NOUN RULES OF ACCENT

10. The accent stays on the same syllable as in the nominative singular so far as the general rules of accent will allow. The accent on the nominative singular must be learned with each word as a pure matter of memory.

11. A long genitive or dative ending, if it has the accent, must have a circumflex.

12. The genitive plural of the first declension always has a circumflex on the ultima (δοξῶν from δόξα).

13. Monosyllabic words of the third declension accent the ultima in the genitive and dative cases (νύξ, νυκτός— not νύκτος).

The noun rules of accent apply also to pronouns, adjectives, and participles.

13

PROCLITICS

14. Proclitics are small words that lean upon the front (πρό and κλίνω) of the following words. Most of them are short prepositions; the fact that a word is a proclitic must be learned when the word is learned in a vocabulary. Proclitics do not have accents *(ἐν ἀρχῇ)*.

CONTRACTING SYLLABLES

15. When two syllables contract into one, if the first of the contracting syllables had an accent, the contracted syllable will have a circumflex (e.g., *ποιέομεν* contracts to *ποιοῦμεν)*; if the second of the contracting syllables had the accent, the contracted syllable keeps the same accent.

ENCLITICS

16. Enclitics are short, unemphatic words or forms that must be learned from the vocabularies or the paradigms. An enclitic leans on *(ἐν* and *κλίνω)* the preceding word. Usually the enclitic will have no accent of its own, but it may change the accent of the word preceding it.

17. If the word preceding the enclitic has an acute on the ultima, it does not change it to a grave *(ἀδελφός ἐστιν)*.

18. If the word preceding the enclitic has an acute on the antepenult or a circumflex on the penult, it acquires an acute on the ultima *(θάλασσά ἐστιν* and *λῦσόν μοι)*.

19. If the word preceding a two-syllable enclitic has an acute on its penult, the enclitic will have an acute (or grave in a sentence unless followed by a mark of punctuation) on its ultima *(τούτῳ ἐστίν)*.

20. If the writer or speaker desires to emphasize a word that is normally an enclitic, he will place an accent upon it and treat it as if it were not an enclitic. If the enclitic comes first in the sentence it always has enough emphasis to have an accent.

14

21. If an enclitic follows a proclitic or another enclitic, the preceding word receives an acute on its ultima.

22. *Οὐκ ἔστιν* is correct, though the normal accented form of the word is *ἐστίν*.

CHAPTER III

PUNCTUATION

The period is the same in form and usage as in English.

The comma is the same in form and virtually the same in usage as in English.

The question mark is the same in usage as in English, but in form it is like an English semicolon (;).

The colon is a dot above the line (·); it does duty for the English colon and semicolon.

Quotation marks are not used. Some editors will start a direct quotation with a capital letter.

The earliest manuscripts did not have any punctuation, and even the later manuscripts differed widely among themselves in regard to punctuation. It is the privilege of each editor and each interpreter to use any punctuation that will fit the context. The student may be sure that the punctuation used in his printed Greek text is good, but he should feel free to change it. This will not give him as much freedom as he might suppose, because usually the context will allow only one possible punctuation.

CHAPTER IV

THE FORMS OF NOUNS

In handling nouns, the student must know the meaning of the word, which may be ascertained from a dictionary. Then he must recognize the form of the noun, which may be found in one of the paradigms. Finally he must know what is indicated by each feature of the form—gender, number, and case. All three steps are absolutely necessary; as the student gains greater familiarity with the language, he will tend to take the steps more and more automatically. In a grammar we deal with the last two steps. First we shall deal with the paradigms.

The Greek language has three declensions, and each of the declensions has further subdivisions.

Section 1

The First Declension

This declension is sometimes called the "a" declension because of the prominence of alpha in its endings.

All words in this declension, except a small group to be discussed below, are feminine in gender.

In the plural, there is only one set of endings for all classes of nouns in this declension. There are some variations in the singular.

Notice that the accent on the genitive plural is always a circumflex on the ultima; this is, of course, an exception to the regular rules for noun accent.

The following three paradigms will handle the vast majority of first declension nouns.

Singular

Nom.	δόξα (glory)	τιμή (honor)	χώρα (place)
Gen.	δόξης	τιμῆς	χώρας
Dat.	δόξῃ	τιμῇ	χώρᾳ
Acc.	δόξαν	τιμήν	χώραν
Voc.	δόξα	τιμή	χώρα

Plural

N.V.	δόξαι	τιμαί	χῶραι
Gen.	δοξῶν	τιμῶν	χωρῶν
Dat.	δόξαις	τιμαῖς	χώραις
Acc.	δόξας	τιμάς	χώρας

The student should get into the habit of breaking down a word into its component parts. He will get the meaning of the word from its root. Then he should recognize the various endings and come to know what is indicated by each ending.

The plural endings of the first declension are always easy to recognize—αι, ων, αις, and ας.

The singular endings are a bit more complex—α or η, ας or ης, ᾳ or η, αν or ην, and α or η. Words that start with η use the η form throughout the singular. Words starting with the α following an ε, ι, or ρ will keep the alpha form throughout the singular, like χώρα. Other words starting with α use the ης and η forms in the genitive and dative singular, like δόξα.

There are a few masculine words of the first declension that act as follows:

Singular

Nom.	στρατιώτης (soldier)	νεανίας (young man)
Gen.	στρατιώτου	νεανίου
Dat.	στρατιώτῃ	νεανίᾳ
Acc.	στρατιώτην	νεανίαν
Voc.	στρατιῶτα	νεανία

Plural

N.V.	στρατιῶται	νεανίαι
Gen.	στρατιωτῶν	νεανιῶν
Dat.	στρατιώταις	νεανίαις
Acc.	στρατιώτας	νεανίας

It will be noticed that these words differ from other words of the first declension only in the nom. and gen. sing. The nom. sing. endings are ης or ας (like the gen. sing. of the first declension feminines). The gen. sing. ending is ου (like the gen. sing. of the second declension).

The alpha endings follow ε, ι, or ρ; otherwise the eta endings are used.

Section 2

The Second Declension

This declension is sometimes called the "o" declension as it makes much use of the o sound in its endings.

Gender is easy to handle in this declension. Words ending in -ος are, with a very few exceptions, masculine. Those with the ending -ον are neuter.

Two simple paradigms will handle the vast majority of second declension nouns.

	Masculine	Neuter

Singular

	Masculine	Neuter
Nom.	λόγος (word)	δῶρον (gift)
Gen.	λόγου	δώρου
Dat.	λόγῳ	δώρῳ
Acc.	λόγον	δῶρον
Voc.	λόγε	δῶρον

Plural

	Masculine	Neuter
N.V.	λόγοι	δῶρα
Gen.	λόγων	δώρων
Dat.	λόγοις	δώροις
Acc.	λόγους	δῶρα

19

Although the vocative has a special ending in the masculine singular, the form of the nominative singular is often used for the vocative.

The student should be able to recognize well the endings of this declension. The masculine endings are: ος, ου, ῳ, ον, ε and οι, ων, οις, ους.

The neuter endings are much the same: ον, ου, ῳ, ον, ον and α, ων, οις, α. It will be noted that all neuter nouns have the same endings for the nominative, accusative and vocative forms—ον for the singular and α for the plural in the second declension.

There are a very few words of the second declension that are feminine. They are declined exactly like the masculines, so no special paradigm need be given. The gender of these nouns will be indicated in the dictionaries. Strikingly, three of the most common of these nouns are found in one verse, Mk. 1:3: ἔρημος, ὁδός and τρίβος. Others found in the N.T. are ἄμμος, ἄμπελος and ῥαβδός. Ἄβυσσος, βάτος, and δόκος are sometimes treated as feminines and sometimes as masculines.

Section 3

The Third Declension

This is often called the consonant declension.

This is by all odds the most difficult of the three declensions. All three genders are found. The endings vary somewhat. Then there are many complications in joining the endings to the various kinds of roots. Only the large grammars can give enough paradigms to handle all the forms found in the N.T., but the paradigms that will be given here will be sufficient for all practical purposes.

It is especially important that the student learn the regular endings of this declension. Then he can develop the ability to spot them in even the more unusual forms, when they may be camouflaged by contractions or unusual ways of uniting with the root.

20

As the vocative case is nearly always the same as the nominative, even in the singular, they will be uniformly presented together. In the few cases where different forms are used, they can be easily recognized in their contexts; they will usually be just a little shorter in form than the nominative singular (e.g., πάτερ from πατήρ).

The masculine and feminine endings of the third declension are:

	Sing.	Plur.
N.V.	ς or —	ες
Gen.	ος	ων
Dat.	ι	σι(ν)
Acc.	α or ν	ας

The dative plural of the third declension may have the ν-movable.

The neuter endings are:

	Sing.	Plur.
N.A.V.	ς or —	α
Gen.	ος	ων
Dat.	ι	σι(ν)

In learning third declension nouns the student must get into the habit of learning the nominative singular, the genitive singular, the gender, and the meaning of the word. If he knows only the nominative singular, seldom can he figure out the other forms. But if he also knows the genitive singular he can ascertain the root, normally by dropping the genitive ending; then he can get the other forms rather well by adding the appropriate endings. There will be some difficulties even so, particularly with the dative plural.

Let us look at a number of typical third declension nouns. If the student becomes familiar with these, he can at least come very close to determining the even more unusual forms when he meets them.

21

ἄρχων, ἄρχοντος, ὁ, ruler:

	Sing.	Plur.
N.V.	ἄρχων	ἄρχοντες
Gen.	ἄρχοντος	ἀρχόντων
Dat.	ἄρχοντι	ἄρχουσι(ν)
Acc.	ἄρχοντα	ἄρχοντας

We see the stem as ἄρχοντ-. The τ is dropped and the vowel is lengthened in the nom. sing. As often in the dat. plur., there is a kind of contraction, -οντσι becoming -ουσι. The other forms are quite regular.

χείρ, χειρός, ἡ, hand:

	Sing.	Plur.
N.V.	χείρ	χεῖρες
Gen.	χειρός	χειρῶν
Dat.	χειρί	χερσί(ν)
Acc.	χεῖρα	χεῖρας

Here we see a slightly peculiar form in the dat. plur. We see also the special accent rule for monosyllables of the third declension, the accent being on the ultima in the gen. and dat.

νύξ, νυκτός, ἡ, night:

	Sing.	Plur.
N.V.	νύξ	νύκτες
Gen.	νυκτός	νυκτῶν
Dat.	νυκτί	νυξί(ν)
Acc.	νύκτα	νύκτας

Notice the difference between the nom. sing. and gen. sing., the monosyllabic accent rule, and the contracted dat. plur. The υ is short, so it does not have a circumflex at any time.

πόλις, πόλεως, ἡ, city:

	Sing.	Plur.
N.V.	*πόλις*	*πόλεις*
Gen.	*πόλεως*	*πόλεων*
Dat.	*πόλει*	*πόλεσι(ν)*
Acc.	*πόλιν*	*πόλεας* or *πόλεις*

The gen. sing. was formerly *πόληος*, and the accent remained the same when the vowels were changed to make *πόλεως*; by a false analogy, then, the accent on the gen. plur. became *πόλεων*. The acc. sing. has the more unusual *ν* rather than *α*. The nom. plur. has contraction, so that the *ες* does not show plainly. The acc. plur. often uses the same form as the nom.

βασιλεύς, βασιλέως, ὁ, king:

	Sing.	Plur.
N.V.	*βασιλεύς*	*βασιλεῖς*
Gen.	*βασιλέως*	*βασιλέων*
Dat.	*βασιλεῖ*	*βασιλεῦσι(ν)*
Acc.	*βασιλέα*	*βασιλέας*

Notice again the peculiar ending of the gen. sing. from an old -*ηος*. Some of the other forms show contractions.

γυνή, γυναικός, ἡ, woman:

	Sing.	Plur.
N.V.	*νυνή*	*γυναῖκες*
Gen.	*γυναικός*	*γυναικῶν*
Dat.	*γυναικί*	*γυναιξί(ν)*
Acc.	*γυναῖκα*	*γυναῖκας*

There is quite a jump from the nom. sing. to the gen. sing. Thereafter the endings are added to the stem quite regularly. The accent, though, acts as if the word had been a monosyllable of the third declension.

23

πατήρ, πατρός, ὁ, father:

	Sing.	Plur.
N.V.	πατήρ	πατέρες
Gen.	πατρός	πατέρων
Dat.	πατρί	πατράσι(ν)
Acc.	πατέρα	πατέρας

This may be called a syncopated noun, because a syllable is omitted (the ε between the τ and ρ) in some of the forms. The dat. plur. ending is a bit strange. The accent acts much like that of the monosyllables. μήτηρ, μητρός, ἡ, mother and θυγάτηρ, θυγατρός, ἡ, sister are declined in the same way.

θρίξ, τριχός, ἡ, hair:

	Sing.	Plur.
N.V.	θρίξ	τρίχες
Gen.	τριχός	τριχῶν
Dat.	τριχί	θριξί(ν)
Acc.	τρίχα	τρίχας

The accent is regular for monosyllables of the third declension. The irregularity is that the θ of the root is not allowed to stand before the χ, as two aspirated sounds coming so close together would not sound good; thus the θ appears only in the N.V. sing. and the dat. plur.

βάπτισμα, βαπτίσματος, τό, baptism:

	Sing.	Plur.
N.V.A.	βάπτισμα	βαπτίσματα
Gen.	βαπτίσματος	βαπτισμάτων
Dat.	βαπτίσματι	βαπτίσμασι(ν)

The student should remember that in the neuter gender, the nom., voc., and acc. forms are always the same, and that in the plural these forms always end in α. The τ of the stem drops out before the σι of the dat. plur.

24

This paradigm will handle most neuter nouns of the third declension when the student knows the nom. and gen. sing.

οὖς, ὠτός, τό, ear:

	Sing.	Plur.
N.V.A.	οὖς	ὦτα
Gen.	ὠτός	ὠτῶν
Dat.	ὠτί	ὠσί(ν)

Notice the very irregular change in the stem and the monosyllabic accent.

πλῆθος, πλήθους, τό, crowd:

	Sing.	Plur.
N.V.A.	πλῆθος	πλήθη(-θεσα)
Gen.	πλήθους(-θεσος)	πληθῶν(-θέσων)
Dat.	πλήθει(-θεσι)	πλήθεσι(ν) (-θεσσι)

The forms in parentheses show the uncontracted forms, which do not occur, but which explain the forms that are in actual use. The ς of the stem drops out, and the vowels contract. The accent is regular for contracting syllables.

Thus we have seen quite a number of third declension nouns. To give the full story in all of its details would almost require a separate paradigm for each noun. The student who has made a careful study of the paradigms and explanations that have been given ought to be able to handle the reading of the third declension nouns with great accuracy. The larger lexicons will give help in dealing with the more irregular forms.

Section 4

Nouns from Other Languages

The New Testament has many nouns taken from other languages, especially from Hebrew, Aramaic, and Latin. When these are brought over into Greek they may be handled in various ways.

Some of them will fit, sometimes with slight adaptation, into one of the regular Greek declensions; e.g., *Μαρία* is a regular first declension; *Παῦλος*, a regular second; and *Σίμων, Σίμωνος*, a regular third.

Many of these foreign words are declined very irregularly; e.g., *Ἰησοῦς, Ἰησοῦ, Ἰησοῦ, Ἰησοῦν, Ἰησοῦ*. The student will soon become familiar with some of the most common words of this class; the others can be found in the dictionaries.

Some of these nouns are simply treated as indeclinables, the same form being used for all cases; e.g., *Ἰερουσαλήμ*.

These borrowed words may be common nouns as well as proper ones; e.g., *κεντυρίων, λεγεών, συνέδριον*.

As languages do not have just the same alphabets or sounds, sometimes the word in Greek will not closely resemble the original; e.g., the Greek *Ἰησοῦς* is quite different from its Hebrew Joshua. At times this may be the source of confusion as the New Testament is compared with the Old.

CHAPTER V

THE GRAMMATICAL USAGE OF NOUNS

When the student has recognized the form of a noun he must then determine the meaning of each feature of that form.

Section 1

Gender

The Greek language has three genders—masculine, feminine, and neuter. There is only a slight correlation between male and masculine, female and feminine, and inanimate and neuter. Gender cannot be ignored, however, as adjectives and pronouns must have the same gender as the nouns with which they are connected. The student may remember that most first declension nouns are feminine; most second declensions in -os are masculine; and all second declensions in -ον are neuter. He will soon become familiar with a few small classes within the third declension that will indicate their genders, but most of the genders of third declension nouns must be learned by rote.

Section 2

Number

The Greek of the New Testament period has only two numbers, singular and plural, for one and for more than one. In the Homeric period there were many examples of the dual number for two things. That luxury number was almost gone in the Classical period, and is not found at all in the New Testament.

Number acts in Greek almost exactly as it does in English.

Adjectives and pronouns must agree in number with the nouns with which they are connected.

Verbs must have the same number as their subjects.

In the case of a compound subject, the verb is usually plural, but it may be singular if the nearest or most important element of the subject is singular, or if the two elements are so closely connected that they may be thought of as a unit.

If the subject is a neuter plural, the verb may be singular or plural. We know no reason for this usage, which has no parallel in English.

If the subject is a collective noun the verb may be singular or plural, depending upon whether the writer or speaker wishes to emphasize the group as a whole or the different elements within the group. This is, of course, the same as in English.

Section 3

Case

When the student has determined the case of the noun with which he is working, he must then seek to determine what the case means in this particular context. All of the cases except the vocative have a number of different usages. The student must seek to choose from all the uses of that case the particular use that will best fit the context of his passage. Usually only one use will fit a context. At times two or more uses will fit equally well, and then the interpretation becomes ambiguous. A passage that may seem perfectly clear in an English translation may really be ambiguous in the Greek. Then a passage that may be ambiguous in the English may be quite clear in Greek. Of course, the Greek is the original, authoritative language of the New Testament, so the honest interpreter should seek to make clear what is clear in the original and should avoid claims of certainty which the ambiguity of the original does not justify. All of this is true for all languages. Actually Greek, with its five cases, has less room for ambiguity in this area than English, with only three cases.

Eight cases are found in Sanskrit, and it is probable that the parent Indo-Germanic language had at least that many

28

cases. Some modern grammarians use the eight cases in New Testament Greek. There might be some excuse for that if each of the eight cases could be boiled down to one usage, but such is not the case. The Greeks had endings for only five cases, just as English has them for only three. Greek is difficult enough at best; there is no profit in making it more difficult by importing difficulties from related languages.

Apposition

Nouns that are in apposition must be in the same case, so we shall not include apposition as a special usage under each case. This is a fundamental rule of language in general.

From time to time the author of the Book of Revelation violates this rule, as he does also other basic grammatical rules. The student can recognize these anacolutha when they occur if he knows the correct usage. The actual meaning is usually just as clear as if the grammar had been perfectly in order. The meaning of the English, "I ain't done nothing nohow," is quite clear, though it lacks something of being good grammar. There are a few other places in the New Testament where the grammar may be suspect, but only in Revelation do we have numerous examples of clear grammatical trouble.

The Nominative Case

1. The Subject of a Finite Verb (the infinitive will use the accusative as its subject). This is a very simple usage found in all languages. τὸ φῶς ἐν τῇ σκοτίᾳ φαίνει, Jn. 1:5: "The light shines in the darkness." The verb may be in any mood except the infinitive; questions, commands and all sorts of sentences as well as simple declarative sentences use this construction.

2. The Predicate Nominative. Here the nominative occurs after the verb "to be" or some similar copula, or connecting verb, expressed or understood. ἐγώ εἰμι ἡ θύρα, Jn. 10:9: "I am the door." At times the predicate nominative will be placed before the verb for emphasis. Quite often the verb will

29

be omitted, but usually it may be supplied quite accurately from the context.

3. The Independent Nominative. This is often called the hanging nominative or the nominative absolute. A word that has no real grammatical connection with the sentence structure has to be put in some case, so the nominative is chosen. Ἀποκάλυψις Ἰωάννου, "The Revelation of John."

The Genitive Case

1. Possession. ἑτοιμάσατε τὴν ὁδὸν κυρίου, Mk. 1:3: "Prepare the way of the Lord." This usage may be extended far beyond cases of real ownership in Greek as it is in English: my sister, my church, my country, etc.

2. Description. This is the usage that gave the name genitive to the case (γένος, kind). κηρύσσων βάπτισμα μετανοίας, Mk. 1:4: "Preaching a baptism of repentance." Quite often the genitive of description can be translated as an adjective: a baptism of repentance or a repentance baptism, a house of wood or a wooden house, etc. This usage is a very wide one, as the description may take many forms. One rather common usage is sometimes separated from the descriptive use and made to be a geographical genitive, but it is probably better to think of it as simply describing in reference to geography: ἦλθεν Ἰησοῦς ἀπὸ Ναζαρὲθ τῆς Γαλιλαίας, Mk. 1:9: "Jesus came from Nazareth of Galilee" (the Galilee Nazareth is meant rather than some other one).

3. Relationship. This is closely related to the preceding usage, but it has certain peculiarities that make special treatment advisable. Ἰάκωβος ὁ τοῦ Ζεβεδαίου, Mt. 10:2: "James the son of Zebedee." A person is identified by attaching the name of some relative to him: Zebedee's James rather than some other James. Most often the relationship is that of father and son, but so far as the construction is concerned any relationship may be intended. When a person uses this construction, he knows just what the relationship is and assumes that his reader does too. We know, for example, that James was the son of

Zebedee. At times, though, we do not possess enough of the original context to enable us to be sure as to what relationship was meant, so we must remain in doubt. The *'Ιούδαν 'Ιακώβου* of Lk. 6:16 may be the son of James or the brother of James; if the latter is true, he may be the same as the Judas the brother of James who wrote the epistle that bears his name. When the author wants to make the matter perfectly plain, he can use the word for father, brother, cousin, or whatever the relationship may be, followed by the genitive of possession, as was done in Jude 1: *'Ιούδας . . . ἀδελφὸς δὲ 'Ιακώβου.*

4. Subjective. This genitive follows a noun that has a verbal idea in it. If that noun were turned into an active verb, the subjective genitive would become its subject. *ἀποκαλύπτεται γὰρ ὀργὴ θεοῦ,* Rom. 1:18: "For the wrath of God is revealed." God's wrath means that God is angry.

5. Objective. Again the genitive follows a noun that contains a verbal idea. If that noun were turned into an active verb, the objective genitive would become its object. *ἐάν τις ἀγαπᾷ τὸν κόσμον, οὐκ ἔστιν ἡ ἀγάπη τοῦ πατρὸς ἐν αὐτῷ,* 1 Jn. 2:15: "If anyone loves the world, the love of the Father is not in him." Here the Father is the object of the verbal idea in the noun love, parallel to the accusative world, the object of the verb in the preceding clause.

Only the context can separate between the subjective and objective genitives, which are really handled just alike. At times the most careful study of the context will leave the matter in doubt. The English language has the very same room for ambiguity; "the love of the father" may refer to the child's love for his father or the father's love for his child. The objective and subjective genitives are very easy to translate into English, but at times they are very difficult, if not impossible, to interpret dogmatically.

6. Partitive. *δώσω σοι ἕως ἡμίσους τῆς βασιλείας μου,* Mk. 6:23: "I will give you up to the half of my kingdom." The part may be anything up to the whole itself. This genitive may follow numbers, cardinal or ordinal. This usage is very

31

easily handled by the use of the word "of" in English.

7. Comparison. The genitive of comparison will follow the comparative degree of an adjective or adverb, and the English "than" must be used to translate it. μείζω τούτων ὄψῃ, Jn. 1:50: "You will see greater things than these." At times the genitive of comparison gives rise to ambiguity. In Jn. 21:15 Jesus says to Peter, ἀγαπᾷς με πλέον τούτων; It is easy to translate that, "Do you love me more than these?" But it is now impossible to tell whether Jesus meant "than these others do" or "than you love these other things." Where the Greek wishes to avoid this source of ambiguity it can use a different construction, using the conjunction for "than," ἤ. Quite often, though, the context makes the genitive of comparison perfectly plain.

8. Complementary. Here the genitive is used to complete the idea begun in certain other words, especially adjectives and nouns. οὐ χρείαν ἔχουσιν οἱ ἰσχύοντες ἰατροῦ, Mt. 9:12: "The well have no need of a physician." There are times when this usage is very close to other usages of the genitive or even overlaps them, but the uncertainty will usually not have any important results for purposes of interpretation; e.g., the sense is really the same in the phrase, "leader of the people," whether we consider "people" the complementary, the objective or the possessive genitive.

9. Time (within which). οὗτος ἦλθεν πρὸς αὐτὸν νυκτός, Jn. 3:2: "This one came to him by night." Some time during the night is meant. The dative regularly expresses time at which—"at the ninth hour." The accusative regularly expresses time throughout which—"he slept eight hours." Yet in the *koine* period there arose quite a bit of confusion between the three cases expressing time. If the genitive of time cannot be handled as time within which in a certain context, it may be time at which or throughout which; the datives and accusatives can likewise be confused with each other and with genitives in their temporal relationships.

10. Value. Οὐχὶ δύο στρουθία ἀσσαρίου πωλεῖται; Mt. 10:29:

32

"Are not two sparrows sold for a farthing?" The exact translation of this usage will be determined by the context.

11. Place. There are only a very few examples of this usage. Usually place is indicated by the use of prepositions, but there are a few examples of the simple genitive indicating a local relationship. ἵνα βάψῃ τὸ ἄκρον τοῦ δακτύλου αὐτοῦ ὕδατος, Lk. 16:24: "that he may dip the tip of his finger in water."

12. The Articular Infinitive Expressing Purpose. There are several ways of expressing purpose in Greek, but one of the rather common ways is that of using the genitive of the definite article with the infinitive. μετέβη ἐκεῖθεν τοῦ διδάσκειν καὶ κηρύσσειν, Mt. 11:1: "He went from there for the purpose of teaching and preaching."

13. The Genitive Absolute. Students who know Latin will recognize this usage as the same as the Latin ablative absolute. καὶ καθίσαντος αὐτοῦ προσῆλθαν αὐτῷ οἱ μαθηταὶ αὐτοῦ, Mt. 5:1: "And when he had taken his seat, his disciples came to him." The basic elements of this construction are a noun (or something in its place) and a participle (expressed or clearly implied), both of them being in the genitive case. It is to be noted that the absolute construction is not an integral part of the main sentence structure. If the sentence had been, "Jesus, having taken his seat, began to teach," the absolute construction would not have been used, but rather a participle in the nominative case would have been used to modify the subject. There are times when the absolute construction is used unnecessarily, when the participle could have been tied in with a secondary element in the main sentence, but that is quite unusual.

The genitive absolute can be expanded indefinitely beyond the two fundamental words, but if the student watches his grammatical principles, he can easily understand even the most complex examples. For example, the noun can be modified by adjectives (in the genitive case, of course) or by prepositional phrases. The participle can be modified by adverbs or prepositional phrases, may take an indirect object (dative) or a

33

direct object (accusative) or a predicate construction (the predicate genitive). There may be several nouns or participles joined by conjunctions. At times, especially in the case of the verb "to be," the participle may be omitted, and two nouns alone will appear, the subject and the predicate (or attribute complement) of the genitive absolute.

We must deal next with the problem of translating the genitive absolute into English. We make some use of a nominative absolute construction, so it is possible to turn a Greek genitive absolute into an English nominative absolute. We can translate Mt. 5:1: "He having sat down, his disciples came to him." But that is hardly idiomatic English. That kind of translation becomes increasingly difficult as the absolute construction becomes more complex. Usually it is better to turn a genitive absolute into an English clause of some sort; e.g., "When he had sat down, his disciples came to him." The problem, though, is to know what kind of clause to use. Usually the context will give a clear indication. In Mt. 5:1, it is clear that we should use a simple temporal clause. But there are contexts which indicate just as clearly a causal clause, a concessive clause, or even a conditional clause. If there is no clear indication of anything else, a temporal clause is normally used. In the use of these clauses there is sometimes some uncertainty and ambiguity, so for exactness it may be better to use the more cumbersome nominative absolute in English; at least, ambiguity should be recognized when it really exists.

14. The Object of Certain Verbs. καὶ ἥψατο τῆς χειρὸς αὐτῆς, Mt. 8:15: "And he touched her hand." The accusative is the normal case for the direct object of verbs, but some verbs take the genitive (and some also the dative). We cannot be sure of any reason for this usage, though in at least some cases there may be something of a partitive idea involved (he touched only a part of her hand). Some verbs that take the genitive can also take the accusative without any recognizable difference in meaning. Some of the more common verbs that take genitive objects are: ἐσθίω, πίνω, γεύομαι, πεινάω, διψάω, ἅπτομαι,

τυγχάνω, πειράομαι, ἀκούω, ἄρχω and μιμνήσκω. It is hardly worthwhile for the student to try to remember such a list, though after a while some of them will fix themselves in his memory. The context will usually make this usage clear. In cases of doubt, the dictionary will always indicate those verbs that take their objects in cases other than the accusative.

15. The Object of Certain Prepositions. This is one of the most common uses of the genitive. Some prepositions, such as ἀπό and ἐκ always take the genitive as their objects. Other prepositions take the genitive and one or two other cases as well, nearly always with different meanings; e.g. μετά with the genitive means "with"; with the accusative, "after." Whenever a student learns a preposition, he should also learn the case or cases used with it as well as the meaning or meanings. All of this is more fully treated in the dictionaries, but the fact of the usage must be noted in a grammar. The student may profitably notice that prepositions denoting separation regularly take the genitive case, but they are by no means the only ones that do.

The Dative Case

1. The Indirect Object. οἱ δὲ εἶπαν αὐτῷ, Jn. 1:38: "And they said to him." The preposition "to" is not always used in English in this construction; in "Give me the book," "me" is, of course, the indirect object, and "book" the direct.

2. Means or Instrument. χάριτί ἐστε σεσῳσμένοι, Eph. 2:5: "By grace are you saved." The prepositions "by" and "with" are usually used to translate this usage into English. This construction is regularly used with impersonal means or instruments, and another construction, ὑπό with the genitive, for personal agents; but in the *koine* period this distinction is not uniformly observed, so at times we find the dative used with persons, and ὑπό and the genitive used with things.

3. Measure. πόσῳ μᾶλλον ὁ πατὴρ ὑμῶν ὁ ἐν τοῖς οὐρανοῖς δώσει ἀγαθὰ τοῖς αἰτοῦσιν αὐτόν, Mt. 7:11: "How much more will your heavenly Father give good things to those that ask

35

him." A more literal but awkward translation would be, "more by how much."

4. Personal Interest. This is often called the ethical dative. τὸ οὖν ἀγαθὸν ἐμοὶ ἐγένετο θάνατος; Rom. 7:13: "Did the good thing, then, become death for me?" Like the indirect object, this usage is usually translated into English by "to" or "for."

5. Respect. ἤμην δὲ ἀγνοούμενος τῷ προσώπῳ ταῖς ἐκκλησίαις, Gal. 1:22: "I was unknown by (or in respect to) face to the churches." Other simple illustrations in English would be: "He was a Jew by race"; "He was dark in color."

6. Time (at which). εἰ ἤδει ὁ οἰκοδεσπότης ποίᾳ φυλακῇ ὁ κλέπτης ἔρχεται, Mt. 24:43: "If the master had known at what watch the thief would come." Let us remember, though, that in the *koine* period there is laxity in the use of the cases used for time; the dative at times means time within which or time throughout which.

7. Possession. This is somewhat different from the possessive genitive. The dative usually follows the verb "to be," expressed or understood. ὄνομα αὐτῷ Ἰωάννης, Jn. 1:6: "Name to him was John." It is normally best to rephrase the construction in English and use the verb "have" or a possessive word. "He had a name John," or "His name was John."

8. Complementary. Like the genitive, the dative is often used to complete the idea begun by certain nouns or adjectives. ὁ γὰρ ἐν τούτῳ δουλεύων τῷ Χριστῷ εὐάρεστος τῷ θεῷ, Rom. 14:18: "For the one who serves Christ in this is well pleasing to God." The student will gradually come to know the words that call for this complementary dative; a dictionary will give him help about individual words when he may be in doubt.

9. Manner. The dative of a noun is used instead of an adverb of manner. δείραντες ἡμᾶς δημοσίᾳ, Acts 16:37: "When they had scourged us publicly."

10. The Object of Certain Verbs. Quite a few verbs take the dative instead of the accusative as their objects. οἱ δὲ εὐθέως ἀφέντες τὰ δίκτυα ἠκολούθησαν αὐτῷ Mt. 4:20: "And they immediately leaving their nets followed him." Most

compound verbs tend to take their objects in the dative. The student will gradually become familiar with verbs that use the dative; the dictionary will give him help with individual verbs. Some verbs take either the dative or the accusative.

11. The Object of Certain Prepositions. εἴδομεν γὰρ αὐτοῦ τὸν ἀστέρα ἐν τῇ ἀνατολῇ, Mt. 2:2: "For we have seen his star in the east." Prepositions denoting rest at a place tend to take the dative, but they are by no means the only ones. The student should learn the case taken by prepositions when he learns the prepositions.

The Accusative Case

1. The Direct Object. εἶδεν πνεῦμα θεοῦ καταβαῖνον, Mt. 3:16: "He saw the Spirit of God coming down." This very common usage is usually very simple to handle, but there are a few complications of it that should be noted.

At times the Greek uses a false passive construction. For example, the active construction is: "John gave me a book." The true passive makes the direct object the subject: "A book was given to me by John." The false passive makes the indirect object the subject and keeps the direct object as the direct object of the passive verb: "I was given a book by John." οἰκονομίαν πεπίστευμαι, I Cor. 9:17: "I have been entrusted with a stewardship."

At times the object will be a noun that has the same root as the verb. This is often called the cognate accusative. It is used for emphasis. ἰδόντες δὲ τὸν ἀστέρα ἐχάρησαν χαρὰν μεγάλην σφόδρα, Mt. 2:10: "And seeing the star they rejoiced a great joy exceedingly."

There are times when a verb will take two objects. This may be called a double accusative. ἠρώτων αὐτὸν οἱ περὶ αὐτὸν σὺν τοῖς δώδεκα τὰς παραβολάς, Mk. 4:10: "Those about him with the twelve asked him the parables." When such a construction is turned into a passive, one of the accusatives may remain an accusative as the object of the passive verb. But in cases like "He made them disciples," the passive would be

37

"They were made disciples," and "disciples" would be a predicate nominative.

2. The Subject of an Infinitive. καὶ συνάγεται πρὸς αὐτὸν ὄχλος πλεῖστος, ὥστε αὐτὸν εἰς πλοῖον ἐμβάντα καθῆσθαι, Mk. 4:1: "And a very great crowd comes to him, so that him, having entered into a boat, to sit down." Often, as here, a literal translation makes very bad English style, so the sentence should be rephrased: " . . . so that he entered into a boat and sat down." The infinitive construction is used much more frequently in Greek than in English.

3. Time (throughout which). καὶ νηστεύσας ἡμέρας τεσσεράκοντα, Mt. 4:2: "And having fasted forty days." Remember that the three cases expressing time are often used laxly in the koine period; the accusative can be used for time at which or within which, though it usually has its most exact meaning of time throughout which.

4. Specification. The Greek at times uses the accusative of specification where we might have expected a dative. βαπτισθέντες τὸ βάπτισμα Ἰωάννου, Lk. 7:29: " . . . baptized with (or in respect to) the baptism of John." γυνὴ περιβεβλημένη τὸν ἥλιον, Rev. 12:1: "A woman clothed with the sun." In English a preposition should be used to translate this usage.

5. The Adverbial Accusative. Often the Greek makes an adverb out of the accusative of a noun, pronoun or adjective. καὶ ῥίψαν αὐτὸν τὸ δαιμόνιον εἰς τὸ μέσον ἐξῆλθεν ἀπ᾽ αὐτοῦ μηδὲν βλάψαν αὐτόν, Lk. 4:35: "The demon, having hurled him into the midst, left him, hurting him not at all." In pronouns and adjectives it is normal to use the neuter gender in this construction.

6. The Accusative Absolute. This rare construction is basically the same as the genitive absolute. It is used with the verb "to be" or an impersonal verb. γνώστην ὄντα σε πάντων τῶν κατὰ Ἰουδαίους ἐθῶν, Acts 26:3: " . . . since you are an expert in Jewish customs." *and h journeyed to a*

7. The Object of Certain Prepositions. ἐπορεύθη εἰς ἔρημον τόπον. The prepositions, the cases they take, and their meanings

should be carefully learned together. Prepositions indicating motion toward a place take the accusative, but so do many others. Some prepositions that take the accusative also take the genitive or dative, usually with different meanings.

The Vocative Case

1. Address. πάτερ, εἰς χεῖράς σου παρατίθεμαι τὸ πνεῦμά μου, Lk. 23:46: "Father, into thy hands I commend my spirit." This is the only use of the vocative case. It is easy to recognize a vocative, even when the form itself is not immediately recognized, because it will always be set off from the rest of the sentence by commas.

Desert place

CHAPTER VI

ADJECTIVES

As adjectives must agree with the nouns they modify in gender, number and case, all three must be shown in the paradigms.

The most common type of adjective is declined:

	Masc.	Fem.	Neut.
		Sing.	
Nom.	ἀγαθός	ἀγαθή	ἀγαθόν
Gen.	ἀγαθοῦ	ἀγαθῆς	ἀγαθοῦ
Dat.	ἀγαθῷ	ἀγαθῇ	ἀγαθῷ
Acc.	ἀγαθόν	ἀγαθήν	ἀγαθόν
Voc.	ἀγαθέ	ἀγαθή	ἀγαθόν
		Plur.	
N.V.	ἀγαθοί	ἀγαθαί	ἀγαθά
Gen.	ἀγαθῶν	ἀγαθῶν	ἀγαθῶν
Dat.	ἀγαθοῖς	ἀγαθαῖς	ἀγαθοῖς
Acc.	ἀγαθούς	ἀγαθάς	ἀγαθά

There is really nothing new to learn here. The masculine column is simply the masculine of the second declension, like λόγος. The feminine is the feminine of the first declension, like τιμή; if the letter before the ending is ε, ι, or ρ, the α endings will be used, as in χώρα. The neuter is the neuter of the second declension, like δῶρον. Such adjectives of three endings are indicated in the dictionaries: ἀγαθός, -η, -ον and ἱερός, -α, -ον.

ἄλλος, ἄλλη, ἄλλο is typical of a small class of adjectives exactly like the former except that in the neuter the nominative, accusative, vocative form is ἄλλο instead of ἄλλον as might have been expected.

ὁ, ἡ, τό, the definite article, "the," is declined:

	Masc.	Fem.	Neut.
		Sing.	
N.V.	ὁ	ἡ	τό
Gen.	τοῦ	τῆς	τοῦ
Dat.	τῷ	τῇ	τῷ
Acc.	τόν	τήν	τό
		Plur.	
N.V.	οἱ	αἱ	τά
Gen.	τῶν	τῶν	τῶν
Dat.	τοῖς	ταῖς	τοῖς
Acc.	τούς	τάς	τά

The forms using the rough breathing instead of the τ are the nominatives, masculine and feminine; they are the proclitics also (having no accents). Note τό in the neuter singular, nominative, accusative and vocative, like ἄλλο.

Other combinations are also found:

The third declension, in many of its forms, is used instead of the first or second. These forms may be ascertained by use of the noun paradigms of that declension.

Some adjectives do not have different forms for all three genders. Two-ending adjectives use the same forms for masculine and feminine and the different forms for the neuter. A few adjectives use the same forms for all genders.

There are a few indeclinable adjectives, such as most of the numerals.

When the student learns an adjective he should learn all the genders as well as the meaning. ἀγαθός, -η, -ον, good, will enable him to handle the word; ἀγαθός, good, will leave him at a loss. When the nominative forms of all genders are known, the student can usually see quickly which noun paradigm to use for each of the genders. Where more unusual forms of the third declension are used, the dictionary will usually give sufficient help to the student to enable him to handle them.

Then, practically, the student can get help in identifying difficult adjectives by noting the forms of the nouns with which they are used.

Comparison of Adjectives

The comparative degree of adjectives is regularly formed by dropping the ς of the masculine nominative singular and adding -τερος, -α, -ον, which is declined like a regular three-ending adjective (the feminine using the α endings after ρ, of course).

The superlative degree is regularly formed by dropping the ς of the masculine nominative singular and adding -τατος, -η, -ον, which is declined like ἀγαθός, -η, -ον.

Many rather common adjectives are compared irregularly, like the English "good, better, best." For example, the comparative degree of ἀγαθός is κρείσσων, -ον (a two-ending third declension); the superlative is κράτιστος, -η, -ον. The irregular forms will be found in the dictionaries. The student need not try to learn a list of them all, but he will gradually become familiar with the most common forms. Many of the irregular comparatives will have the endings -ων, -ον or -ιων, -ιον; many of the superlatives, -ιστος, -η, -ον.

The comparative degree, in Greek as in English, is regularly used when only two persons or things are involved; the superlative, when more than two. In the *koine* period, however, this distinction was not always observed, even by the most careful writers.

After the comparative degree, the genitive of comparison may be used or the conjunction ἤ (meaning "than") followed by whatever case the context may demand. The latter usage is usually more definite, though often the former is made quite clear by the context.

The superlative degree is often followed by the partitive (or complementary) genitive. It may be followed by a prepositional phrase, or it may stand alone. At times the superlative has the meaning of "very" instead of "most"; e.g., "very great" instead of "greatest." The context must determine which translation is to be preferred.

Usages of Adjectives

Adjectives may be used as direct modifiers of nouns. ὅτι πόλις ἐστὶν τοῦ μεγάλου βασιλέως, Mt. 5:35: "For it is the city of the great king." The article is, of course, an adjective; it will have some special treatment below. Both τοῦ and μεγάλου modify the noun βασιλέως.

Adjectives agree with the nouns they modify in gender, number and case. Quite often this will make the adjective and its noun have the same ending; this need not be true, though, as different declensions and paradigms may be involved, as in the case of τοῦ μεγάλου βασιλέως.

There is somewhat more flexibility in the order of words than in English. Three attributive positions are recognized. The most common is, as in English, ὁ ἀγαθὸς ἄνθρωπος. The second is also rather common, ὁ ἄνθρωπος ὁ ἀγαθός. The third is rather rare, ἄνθρωπος ὁ ἀγαθός--"A man, the good one I mean." If an article is not used, the adjective usually precedes the noun it modifies, but it may also follow it.

Adjectives may be in the predicate position, following the verb "to be" or some equivalent. μακάριος εἶ, Mt. 16:17: "Blessed are you." Such predicate adjectives must also agree with the noun or pronoun with which they are connected in gender, number and case. In this example, μακάριος is nom. sing. masc. in agreement with the "you" implied in the verb as its subject.

The predicate adjective usually follows its verb, but for the sake of emphasis it may be placed before the verb or even before the subject of the verb.

The Definite Article

The New Testament Greek does not have the indefinite article, "a" or "an," so the student has the right to use it or not in English, according to his knowledge of the context and of English idiom.

Greek does have the definite article, "the," ὁ, ἡ, τό.

The use of the Greek definite article is roughly the same as that in English, so the student will start by trying to use a "the" whenever he has a form of the Greek article.

But unfortunately the matter is not that simple. The great Classical Greek grammarian, Gildersleeve, devoted most of the second volume of his grammar to the treatment of the article in Classical Greek; not all of that would be applicable to the New Testament, of course; but quite a few special pages would be necessary for some idioms found in the New Testament that he did not need to handle for Classical Greek. We shall call attention to some of the most important differences between our English usage of the article and that found in *koine* Greek. The student is urged to go very slowly and carefully in his handling of the definite article in his interpretation of the New Testament. There are times when the presence or absence of the article may be very significant, but the student should be sure of his position before becoming too dogmatic about it. The serious student will want to watch the use of the article as he reads the New Testament; little by little he will find himself appreciating the Greek usage and being able to understand it and use it as a tool of interpretation. He will wish to study the larger grammars and the better critical commentaries as he goes more deeply into the matter.

The Greek often uses the article with proper names. Usually we can discern no difference in meaning whether the article is present or not. We should translate either ὁ ʼΙησοῦς or ʼΙησοῦς as "Jesus." In only a few contexts do we seem to have something like "the particular Jesus about whom we have been talking."

The Greek often uses the definite article with abstract nouns, where the English idiom would omit it. In I Cor. 13, "love" is either ἀγάπη or ἡ ἀγάπη.

There are times, though, when the Greek does not have the article but when English idiom demands it. Here is an area where much real common sense is needed. Greek and English are not identical languages; most of us know English idiom rather well, and we should seek to develop as good a knowledge of the Greek idiom here as possible.

The matter is complicated for us by the fact that most of the authors of the N.T. books were Jews, and their use of the Greek article was influenced by their knowledge of the Hebrew of the O.T. and the related Aramaic, their primary language. Here the student of the N.T. will be greatly helped by a knowledge of at least Hebrew. For example, in Hebrew a noun in the construct state (roughly, a noun having a genitive depending upon it) cannot have a definite article with it. So the student may notice how often a noun followed by a genitive will not have an article in the N.T., though the English idiom may require it, and the student should put it in in his translation.

There are some rather common special uses of the article with particular words that should be noted.

With αὐτός. The word αὐτός has three quite different meanings. (1) If the article immediately precedes αὐτός it means "the same"; ὁ αὐτὸς ἄνθρωπος or ὁ ἄνθρωπος ὁ αὐτός means "the same man." (2) If the article does not precede an αὐτός with a noun or pronoun, αὐτός becomes an intensive, meaning "-self." ὁ ἄνθρωπος αὐτός is "the man himself"; ἐγὼ αὐτός is "I myself"; and so on. In the nominative case αὐτός can be used as an intensive pronoun, such as "he himself." (3) In cases other than the nominative αὐτός by itself is the unemphatic third person pronoun, "he," "she," "it," or "they."

With οὗτος and ἐκεῖνος. When these words are used as demonstrative adjectives, the definite article must immediately precede the nouns that are modified. For "this man," e.g., the Greek must have οὗτος ὁ ἄνθρωπος or ὁ ἄνθρωπος οὗτος. Quite different is οὗτος ἄνθρωπος, which would mean "This is a man."

With the possessive adjectives, ἐμός, σός, ἡμέτερος, and ὑμέτερος. These are not very often used, but when they are, the definite article must precede the possessive adjective. "My book" is ὁ ἐμὸς βίβλος or ὁ βίβλος ὁ ἐμός. (Much more common would be the use of the genitive case of the personal pronoun, ὁ βίβλος μου.)

45

CHAPTER VII

PRONOUNS

In Greek, as in English, a pronoun is a word that is used in place of a noun.

As pronouns were developed so early in the history of the language, they present many irregularities, particularly in their declensions. They are used so commonly, though, that the student should make the diligent effort to learn them as well as possible.

In general, the pronouns are used in Greek much as they are in English. But as the paradigm for each is presented, attention will be called to special points of usage appropriate to each.

As some Greek pronouns, like adjectives, show gender, number and case, all of these factors must be handled. The pronoun will take its gender and number from the antecedent, or the word for which it stands. But the case will be determined by the pronoun's own usage in the sentence. For example, "The book which I have" is ὁ βίβλος ὃν ἔχω. The pronoun ὅν is masculine singular because βίβλος is, but it is accusative because it is the object of the verb ἔχω.

Personal Pronouns

First person:

	Sing.	Plur.
	Sing.	Plur.
N.V.	ἐγώ	ἡμεῖς
Gen.	ἐμοῦ (μου)	ἡμῶν
Dat.	ἐμοί (μοι)	ἡμῖν
Acc.	ἐμέ (με)	ἡμᾶς

The three forms in parentheses are enclitics, used when no emphasis is intended. ὁ βίβλος μου is "My book," while ὁ βίβλος ἐμοῦ is "*My* book." There is no need for a nominative unemphatic form, as that form is not used unless emphasis is intended; the unemphatic "I" would be simply the first person

46

singular of the verb; e.g. λύω is "I loose," while ἐγὼ λύω is "*I* loose." No distinction is made in the oblique cases of the plural between emphatic and unemphatic forms.

It will be noted that the endings and accents appear quite irregular. There is a mixture of second and third declension endings, and there are some contractions.

Gender is not shown in this pronoun.

Second person:

	Sing.	Plur.
N.V.	σύ	ὑμεῖς
Gen.	σοῦ (σου)	ὑμῶν
Dat.	σοί (σοι)	ὑμῖν
Acc.	σέ (σε)	ὑμᾶς

The second person is much like the first in endings and accents; the plural is exactly the same except for the initial vowel.

The unemphatic forms in parentheses are spelled just like the emphatic forms, but they are enclitics. All that was said about emphasis in the first person applies here.

Third person:

αὐτός, -η, -ο is used for the third personal pronoun. It is declined just like ἀγαθός, -η, -ον except that the neuter singular N.A.V. is αὐτό, not αὐτόν.

It will be noted that αὐτός shows the three genders.

Whenever the nominative form is used it is emphatic and intensive, "-self." In the oblique cases it is regularly unemphatic. When emphasis is intended, a demonstrative pronoun (οὗτος or ἐκεῖνος) is used.

Demonstrative Pronouns

	Masc.	Fem.	Neut.
		Sing.	
N.V.	οὗτος (this)	αὕτη	τοῦτο
Gen.	τούτου	ταύτης	τούτου
Dat.	τούτῳ	ταύτῃ	τούτῳ
Acc.	τοῦτον	ταύτην	τοῦτο

47

Plur.

N.V.	οὗτοι	αὗται	ταῦτα
Gen.	τούτων	τούτων	τούτων
Dat.	τούτοις	ταύταις	τούτοις
Acc.	τούτους	ταύτας	ταῦτα

The endings here are quite regular, except for τοῦτο in the neuter singular N.A.V.

The rough breathing is used in the N.V. of the masculine and feminine; otherwise, τ. (This is just the same as in the definite article, it will be remembered.)

The diphthong of the first syllable is αυ before endings that begin with α; otherwise it is ου.

ἐκεῖνος, -η, -ο, "that," is declined perfectly regularly like ἀγαθός, -η, -ον except for -o in the neuter singular N.A.V.

ὅδε, ἥδε, τόδε ("this") is used very seldom in the New Testament. The first part is declined like the definite article, except that it always has an accent; the -δε stays the same.

The *koine* has developed a similar word, ὅσδε, ἥδε, ὅδε ("this"), with the first part being declined like the relative pronoun and the -δε being unchanged.

οὗτος and ἐκεῖνος may be used as either pronouns or adjectives; for their adjectival use see the adjective section above (p. 40).

Interrogative Pronoun

	Sing.		Plur.	
	Masc. Fem.	Neut.	Masc. Fem.	Neut.
Nom.	τίς (who)	τί	τίνες	τίνα
Gen.	τίνος	τίνος	τίνων	τίνων
Dat.	τίνι	τίνι	τίσι(ν)	τίσι(ν)
Acc.	τίνα	τι	τίνας	τίνα

The endings are those of the third declension.

The accent of the interrogative is always an acute on the first syllable; it does not even change to a grave on τίς and τί when they are followed by other words in a sentence.

Indefinite Pronoun

τις, τι, "someone, something," is declined exactly like the interrogative except for the accent. The indefinite is an enclitic, so it will have no accent at all or whatever may be required by the special accent rules for enclitics.

Relative Pronoun

	Sing.			Plur.		
	Masc.	Fem.	Neut.	Masc.	Fem.	Neut.
N.V.	ὅς	ἥ	ὅ	οἵ	αἵ	ἅ
Gen.	οὗ	ἧς	οὗ	ὧν	ὧν	ὧν
Dat.	ᾧ	ᾗ	ᾧ	οἷς	αἷς	οἷς
Acc.	ὅν	ἥν	ὅ	οὕς	ἅς	ἅ

The student should not allow himself to confuse this with the somewhat similar definite article.

This is made up of the rough breathing and the regular second and first declension endings, except that the neuter singular N.A.V. has the ending -o instead of -ον. All of the accents are perfectly regular.

The student should expect the relative pronoun to agree with its antecedent in gender and number and to get its case from its usage in its own clause. ἐφανέρωσά σου τὸ ὄνομα τοῖς ἀνθρώποις οὓς ἔδωκάς μοι, Jn. 17:6: "I have manifested thy name to the men whom thou gavest me." οὕς is masculine plural in agreement with ἀνθρώποις; it is accusative because it is the object of ἔδωκάς.

There are times, though, when the relative allows its case too to be determined by its antecedent, particularly if the antecedent immediately precedes the relative. This is case by attraction. ὃς δ᾽ ἂν πίῃ ἐκ τοῦ ὕδατος οὗ ἐγὼ δώσω αὐτῷ, Jn. 4:14: "Whoever drinks of the water which I shall give to him."

In a very few cases we have the phenomenon of inverse attraction, where the antecedent is attracted to the case of the relative. It may be questioned as to whether this is really

49

correct grammar or not. ἄγοντες παρ' ᾧ ξενισθῶμεν Μνάσωνί τινι Κυπρίῳ, Acts 21:16: "Bringing a certain Cyprian, Mnason, with whom we might stay." Mnason would normally be accusative as the object of the verb, but here it is dative by attraction to ᾧ.

At times the gender of the relative will be determined by sense rather than by the grammatical gender of the antecedent, particularly if the antecedent is separated rather far from the relative. ... πάντα τὰ ἔθνη ἐφ' οὓς ἐπικέκληται τὸ ὄνομά μου, Acts 15:17: " . . . all the nations upon whom my name has been called."

The Greek quite often omits the antecedent of a relative pronoun if the context clearly implies it. ὃν ἔχεις οὐκ ἔστιν σου ἀνήρ, John 4:18: "(He) whom you have is not your husband."

Indefinite Relative Pronoun

	Masc.	Fem.	Neut.
		Sing.	
N.V.	ὅστις	ἥτις	ὅτι
Gen.	οὗτινος	ἧστινος	οὗτινος
Dat.	ᾧτινι	ᾗτινι	ᾧτινι
Acc.	ὅντινα	ἥντινα	ὅτι
		Plur.	
N.V.	οἵτινες	αἵτινες	ἅτινα
Gen.	ὧντινων	ὧντινων	ὧντινων
Dat.	οἷστισι(ν)	αἷστισι(ν)	οἷστισι(ν)
Acc.	οὕστινας	ἅστινας	ἅτινα

The regular, full meaning of this word is "whoever." In the *koine*, however, it is often used as if it were the relative ὅς, meaning simply "who." At times it seems to have a qualitative idea, "the kind of person who." The student must study each context carefully to try to determine what the word means in that particular context.

It will be noticed that the word is made up of the relative pronoun and the indefinite pronoun, and each part of the word is declined. Not too many of these forms are in actual use in the New Testament, but it is easier to know the whole declension than to try to learn which forms do occur and which do not. At times shorter forms, like ὅτου for the genitive singular masculine, occur.

Reflexive Pronouns

"Myself" is ἐμαυτός, -η, -ον, declined like ἀγαθός, -η, -ον.

"Thyself" is σεαυτός, -η, -ον, declined like ἀγαθός, -η, -ον.

"Himself, herself, itself," is ἑαυτός, -η, -ον, declined like ἀγαθός, -η, -ον.

All of these, of course, are only in the singular.

The plurals for all three persons, "Ourselves, yourselves, themselves," are the same: ἑαυτοί, ἑαυταί, ἑαυτά, declined like the plurals ἀγαθοί, -αι, -α.

At times all the forms beginning with ἑαυτ- are contracted to αὑτ-. Then they are like the corresponding forms of αὐτός except for the rough breathings.

Reciprocal Pronoun

"Each other" or "one another" is expressed by the reciprocal pronoun ἀλλήλων. There is no need for a singular number or a nominative or vocative case, so we start with the genitive plural. The only forms that actually occur in the New Testament are: ἀλλήλων, ἀλλήλοις, and ἀλλήλους. ἐντολὴν καινὴν δίδωμι ὑμῖν, ἵνα ἀγαπᾶτε ἀλλήλους, Jn. 13:34: "A new commandment I give you, that you love one another."

CHAPTER VIII

ADVERBS

As in English, Greek adverbs modify verbs, adjectives or other adverbs.

The most common adverbial ending is -ως, occurring in place of the common adjective ending -ος of the nominative singular masculine.

Another rather common way of making an adverb is to use the neuter singular nominative or accusative form of an adjective, -ον.

Adverbs have no declension, but they do have the phenomenon of comparison: "more slowly," "most slowly." The most common endings are -τερως for the comparative and -τατως for the superlative. Other forms will be found in the dictionaries.

The Negatives Οὐ and Μή

The negative words οὐ and μή are adverbs, but they require special treatment.

Greek has two words for the English "not," οὐ and μή. In Classical Greek it was very difficult to learn when to use one or the other, but in the *koine* period the matter was greatly simplified. Except in questions, the rule is: use οὐ when the indicative mood of the verb is used or implied; otherwise, μή. The student should not be worried as he runs into exceptions to this simple rule; most of the exceptions will be a reflection of the older Classical usage, and there will be no difference in meaning between the two negatives.

In questions, however, the matter is quite different. The two negatives are used to indicate the answer expected for the question asked: οὐ expects a positive answer, and μή a negative.

The positive expectation is easy to translate into English. οὐχ ὑμεῖς μᾶλλον διαφέρετε αὐτῶν; Mt. 6:26: "Are you not much more valuable than they?" We simply put a "not" into the question, and the positive answer is expected.

It is much more difficult to indicate the negative expectation. In speaking, the tone of voice may give the indication. In writing, however, another device must be used; e.g., "That is not so, is it?" Because this is rather cumbersome, nearly all of the common translations of the New Testament simply ignore the μή and ask the question with no indication of the answer expected. There are times when an interesting, if not important, shade of meaning is lost because of this. For example, the Samaritan woman said to the men in John 4:29: μήτι οὗτός ἐστιν ὁ χριστός. This does not mean, as it is often translated, "Is not this the Christ?" The men would probably have answered, "Who are you to be telling us who the Christ is?" The woman used excellent psychology when she said, with a μήτι toning down the μή a bit, "This can't be the Christ, can it?" The men responded to that and came and saw for themselves.

It should be noted, of course, that the answer that is expected is not always received; the questioner has no power to force the answerer to follow his expectation.

οὐ is the form used before words beginning with a consonant; οὐκ, before words beginning with a vowel with a smooth breathing; οὐχ, before words beginning with a vowel with a rough breathing.

Modal Signs

The modal signs ἄν and ἐάν may be considered adverbs. There is no direct translation that can be given for them, but they are necessary in certain constructions, such as certain types of conditional sentences and certain clauses using the subjunctive and optative moods. The signs will be discussed more fully in connection with the constructions themselves.

In Classical Greek the modal sign was simply ἄν; ἐάν was a contraction of εἰ ("if") and ἄν. But often the ἐάν was contracted still further into ἄν, which made it look like the simple modal sign. As ἄν and ἐάν were so closely related even in Classical Greek, it is not surprising when, in the *koine* period, we find ἐάν used just like the simple modal sign as well as being εἰ plus ἄν.

CHAPTER IX

CONJUNCTIONS

Conjunctions in Greek act very much as they do in English, joining words, phrases, clauses and sentences.

Certain conjunctions are integral parts of certain constructions (e.g., ἵνα and purpose clauses), so they will be discussed in connection with the constructions.

Classical Greek had a wealth of small conjunctions (often called particles) that are quite difficult, if not impossible even, to translate into English adequately. Many of those particles did not find their way into the *koine* period and the New Testament. Some of those that did come into the New Testament were not used with the finesse of the Classical period. The student should be careful to study his particles with the help of New Testament dictionaries and commentaries and not depend on the Classical usage alone.

The balancing particles, μέν--δέ and τέ--καί, are still in common use in the New Testament, but quite often the first member is not followed by the second at all. τέ and καί can be easily translated by "both" and "and." But μέν and δέ can hardly be translated without too much emphasis; in speaking, they can be brought out by tones of voice and gestures; in writing, "on the one hand" and "on the other hand" are really too much. It is probably better to leave the μέν out and translate the δέ by an "and" or a "but." With experience, the student will gain the ability to handle these and other particles so that he can at least understand what the Greek is trying to indicate, even if he cannot find an adequate English translation for them.

Postpositive Conjunctions. In general, the position of the conjunctions in Greek is much the same as in English, but there are a few postpositive conjunctions, μέν, δέ, γάρ, οὖν,

55

μέντοι, and γε, that may never be first in their clauses or sentences; they usually come second, but at times they are even further from the first. We must, of course, put the English equivalents in their proper English order when we make a smooth translation.

CHAPTER X

PREPOSITIONS

Like English, Greek has many prepositions. Their use is basically the same in both languages, but certain special points should be noted about the Greek usage.

English has only one case to serve as the object of all prepositions, the accusative or objective. Greek, however, has three cases that are used with prepositions, the genitive, the dative, and the accusative.

Some prepositions take only one of the cases; some, two of them; others, all three. Prepositions that use two or three cases regularly have a difference in meaning as the different cases are used. For example, μετά with the genitive means "with," while with the accusative it means "after." It is necessary, then, that the student in learning the prepositions should learn the cases that are used with them and the meanings with the various cases. As an aid to memory, the student will notice that prepositions denoting separation from a place tend to take the genitive case; those showing rest at a place, the dative; and those indicating motion toward a place, the accusative. Of course, many of the prepositions have nothing to do with place, so the cases used with them must be simply memorized.

Laxity in Meaning of Prepositions

In the *koine* period the prepositions were not always used with the exactitude of the Classical period. People whose mother tongue was not Greek did not use them as carefully as did the natives, particularly those of the literary period of the Classical days. Greek had far more prepositions than Hebrew and Aramaic, so the Jewish authors of the New Testament were embarrassed with the riches of the Greek language in this respect. The student, then, should not depend finally on a dictionary of Classical Greek for the meaning of prepositions in the New Testament but should use a dictionary that deals with the *koine* period, with the bearing of the papyri on the *koine* Greek, and with the specific New Testament usage. Some of the older dictionaries and commentaries are quite weak at this point.

Prepositions With Infinitives

Infinitives are verbal nouns, so it is quite logical that they should be used as the objects of various prepositions. Infinitives are not declined, so the definite article is usually used (in the neuter gender) to show the case. Of course, if there is a subject of the infinitive it will be in the accusative case. This construction can be extended indefinitely. The student should first translate this construction very literally; then, after he has caught the Greek meaning, he should turn it into idiomatic English, usually by the use of a clause of some sort. καὶ μετὰ τὸ παραδοθῆναι τὸν Ἰωάννην ἦλθεν ὁ Ἰησοῦς, Mk. 1:14: "And after the to have been delivered up the John, came Jesus." Then, "And after John had been delivered up, Jesus came."

ἐν with the dative can usually best be handled by a temporal clause introduced by "while"; εἰς with the accusative, by a purpose clause; διά with the accusative, by a causal clause; and so on. This usage may seem strange to the English-speaking student at first, but it is quite logical, and the Greeks were quite fond of it.

"Improper" Prepositions

There are quite a few words that are most commonly used as adverbs that are sometimes used as prepositions. When they are used as prepositions, some grammarians call them "improper" prepositions; others, "adverbs used as prepositions." In a sense, that is quite illogical. If a word is used as a preposition, there is nothing improper about it, and it need not be called an adverb used as a preposition; it simply is a preposition.

There is, however, some advantage in recognizing this group, as virtually all of them take the genitive case as their objects.

Notes

Many of the prepositions are proclitics; that fact should be noticed when the word is learned.

Most of the prepositions ending in a vowel drop the vowel before words beginning with a vowel, and the omission is indicated by an apostrophe; e.g., μετ᾽ αὐτοῦ. Then the consonant before the dropped vowel is often changed before a vowel with a rough breathing; e.g., μεθ᾽ ἑαυτοῦ. So likewise: ἀπό, ἀπ᾽, and ἀφ᾽; ἐπί, ἐπ᾽, and ἐφ᾽; etc.

The meanings of the individual prepositions are given in the exicons, so they need not be discussed in a grammar.

CHAPTER XI

INTERJECTIONS

Interjections in Greek act just like those in English. The only problem for the student is that of learning their meanings from the dictionary.

There are times when there is some difficulty in distinguishing between an interjection and the imperative mood of a verb, but a careful study of the context will usually clarify the matter. For example, ἴδε ὁ ἀμνὸς τοῦ θεοῦ, Jn. 1:29. Here the ἴδε may be either an interjection or an imperative of the verb. But if it had been the imperative in this context we would have had τὸν ἀμνόν, its object in the accusative case; so we know that it is the interjection. It is not "See the lamb of God," but "See, the lamb of God."

Theoretically, interjections have only one form, with no conjugation or declension. But actually some of them that are much like the imperatives of certain verbs do tend to develop just a bit of something like a conjugation; e.g., ἰδού, and ἴδε (singular) and ἴδετε (plural).

Interjections are usually set off by commas in English, but the editors of our Greek texts do not regularly follow that practice.

CHAPTER XII

THE FORMS OF VERBS

Verbs are by all odds the most complex feature of the Greek language. The Greek verb is highly inflected. The student must determine to work diligently in an attempt to come to as near a mastery of the Greek verb as possible. It is in this area that he can expect to get more real benefit from his study of the Greek New Testament than in any other.

We shall first present the numerous paradigms that are necessary to enable the student to recognize the various verb forms that are found in the New Testament. Then we shall study the usages of the various forms.

Most Greek verbs show five different things:

1. Person — first, second and third, just as in English.

2. Number — singular and plural, as in English.

3. Tense — slightly similar to English tense, but to be studied much more fully later.

4. Voice — active, middle and passive. The first and last are much like English, though all three must be studied more fully later.

5. Mood (or mode) — indicative, subjunctive, optative, imperative, infinitive and participle. This is somewhat like English, but it must be studied much more fully later.

The student cannot learn the verb paradigms without much pure memory work, but an attempt will be made to give as much help as possible by showing the student how the various forms are made up and what are the identifying signs of various forms.

The student should get in the habit of breaking down the verb forms and seeing what is indicated by each feature of the form. For example, ἐλύθησαν may be handled thus: The ἐ- is the augment, showing that the form is a past tense of the indicative mood. -λυ- is the root of the verb λύω, meaning "loose." -θη- is a sign of the sixth principal part, an aorist or future passive. -σαν is the third person plural ending of some past tense. Now putting those all together we find that the form is the third, plural, aorist, indicative, passive of λύω, "they were loosed." The more experience the student has in doing this, the more automatic will it all become.

The student should be warned against becoming dependent upon an analytical lexicon for identifying his verb forms. That is like a crutch, and those who lean on it will never learn to walk. There are, of course, certain very difficult verb forms in the New Testament, but nearly all lexicons will give enough analytical help to help the student understand them. Thayer, for example, has an appendix showing the forms of many of the more difficult verbs. Other lexicons will show the more difficult forms in the body of the lexicon.

Unfortunately there are very few completely regular verbs in Greek, so it is necessary to have a large number of paradigms. Then in order to know which paradigm to use for the various verbs, it is necessary to know the principal parts of at least a number of the most common, typical verbs. For example, the principal parts of ἀγγέλλω are: ἀγγέλλω, so the paradigm of the regular λύω is used; ἀγγελῶ, so the paradigm for the liquid future must be used; ἤγγειλα, indicating the paradigm for the liquid aorist; ἤγγελκα, ἤγγελμαι, ἠγγέλθην, indicating that the paradigms for the regular λύω are used for the last three principal parts. All possible combinations are found in the various verbs. Most dictionaries give the principal parts of verbs, or at least those parts that show irregularities. Yet the student will find it most helpful if he memorizes the principal parts of at least thirty or more of the most common irregular verbs.

There are two main conjugations of Greek verbs, the -ω and the -μι, but these distinctions show up clearly only in the forms made under the first principal part. And there are many subdivisions in each of the conjugations, and also under the other principal parts. There can be no simple presentation of all the necessary paradigms. Perhaps the easiest and most logical way will be to take each principal part as the unit and present all the appropriate paradigms under each one.

The paradigms given will handle well over 99 % of all verb forms in the New Testament. An absolutely complete coverage would demand a much larger grammar. The forms not handled by these paradigms will be found usually in the dictionaries under the special words themselves.

Section 1

The First Principal Part

Under the first principal part are found the present and imperfect tenses in all voices.

Present indicative active of the regular verb λύω:

	Sing.	Plur.
1st Person	λύω	λύομεν
2nd ,,	λύεις	λύετε
3rd ,,	λύει	λύουσι(ν)

The present indicative is made up of the present stem, the connecting vowel, and the personal endings. Here, though, contraction has tied the last two elements tightly together, so we should recognize the two together as -ω, -εις, -ει, -ομεν, -ετε, -ουσι(ν). The (ν) on the third person plural ending is the ν moveable.

Present indicative middle or passive of λύω:

	Sing.	Plur.
1	λύομαι	λυόμεθα
2	λύῃ	λύεσθε
3	λύεται	λύονται

Here the middle or passive endings are used: -μαι, -σαι, -ται, -μεθα, -σθε, -νται.

The connecting vowel o/ε is used: o before endings beginning with μ or ν, otherwise ε.

In the second singular there is contraction; the σ of the ending drops out and the ε and $\alpha\iota$ contract to η.

The same forms are used for both middle and passive here.

Present subjunctive active of λύω:

	Sing.	Plur.
1	λύω	λύωμεν
2	λύῃς	λύητε
3	λύῃ	λύωσι(ν)

Present subjunctive middle or passive of λύω:

	Sing.	Plur.
1	λύωμαι	λυώμεθα
2	λύῃ	λύησθε
3	λύηται	λύωνται

The only difference between the subjunctive and the indicative is that the subjunctive uses the long connecting vowel ω/η (ω before μ and ν, elsewhere η). In the active, the connecting vowels and the endings are run together as in the indicative. In the middle/passive there is the contraction in the second singular.

The student can see already that the same form may appear in several places in the paradigms, such as λύω and λύῃ. The context must be studied in an attempt to determine which of the forms is intended; usually no ambiguity will be left when that is done.

Present optative active of λύω:

	Sing.	Plur.
1	λύοιμι	λύοιμεν
2	λύοις	λύοιτε
3	λύοι	λύοιεν

Here we see the present stem, the optative connecting vowel

οι, and a new set of person endings (much like those that we shall see in the -μι verbs): -μι, -ς, --, -μεν, -τε, -εν.

Present optative middle or passive of λύω.

	Sing.	Plur.
1	λυοίμην	λυοίμεθα
2	λύοιο	λύοισθε
3	λύοιτο	λύοιντο

This is made up of the present stem, the optative connecting vowel, and the secondary middle/passive endings: -μην, -σο (with the σ dropping out), -το, -μεθα, -σθε, -ντο. We notice that the optative uses secondary endings, while the subjunctive uses the primary endings.

The optative is not used very often in the New Testament, so the student need not spend much time trying to master it.

Present imperative active of λύω:

	Sing.	Plur.
2	λῦε	λύετε
3	λυέτω	λυέτωσαν

Present imperative middle or passive or λύω:

	Sing.	Plur.
2	λύου	λύεσθε
3	λυέσθω	λυέσθωσαν

There is no first person in the imperative; the hortatory subjunctive takes the place of the first person plural, and there is never any need for a first person singular.

Here we have the present stem, the ο/ε connecting vowel and special imperative endings. The student will not find it easy to remember these forms exactly, as they are not used too often. But when they do occur, the context usually indicates rather clearly that the form is an imperative; then the person and number can rather easily be ascertained.

Present infinitives of λύω:

Active: λύειν. Middle/passive: λύεσθαι.

In the active the connecting vowel and the ending are run together into -ειν. In the middle/passive the connecting vowel is -ε and the ending -σθαι.

Present active participle of λύω:

Sing.

	Masc.	Fem.	Neut.
N.V.	λύων	λύουσα	λῦον
Gen.	λύοντος	λυούσης	λύοντος
Dat.	λύοντι	λυούσῃ	λύοντι
Acc.	λύοντα	λύουσαν	λῦον

Plur.

	Masc.	Fem.	Neut.
N.V.	λύοντες	λύουσαι	λύοντα
Gen.	λυόντων	λυουσῶν	λυόντων
Dat.	λύουσι(ν)	λυούσαις	λύουσι(ν)
Acc.	λύοντας	λυούσας	λύοντα

As a participle is a verbal adjective, the Greek developed a full declension within its verbal paradigm.

Here the connecting vowel is united so closely with the ending of the participle that it is simpler to learn the two together as -ων, -ουσα, -ον, the nominative singular of the three genders. Then the masculine and neuter genders are declined in the third declension, while the feminine uses the first, like δόξα.

Present middle or passive participle of λύω:

	Masc.	Fem.	Neut.
		Sing.	
N.V.	λυόμενος	λυομένη	λυόμενον
Gen.	λυομένου	λυομένης	λυομένου
Dat.	λυομένῳ	λυομένη	λυομένῳ
Acc.	λυόμενον	λυομένην	λυόμενον

66

Plur.

	Sing. / Plur.		
N.V.	λυόμενοι	λυόμεναι	λυόμενα
Gen.	λυομένων	λυομένων	λυομένων
Dat.	λυομένοις	λυομέναις	λυομένοις
Acc.	λυομένους	λυομένας	λυόμενα

Here we see clearly the present stem, the connecting vowel, and the middle/passive participle ending, -μενος, -η, -ον. The masculine and neuter are declined in the second declension, and the feminine in the first, just like the most common adjective, ἀγαθός, -η, -ον.

Imperfect indicative active of λύω:

	Sing.	Plur.
1	ἔλυον	ἐλύομεν
2	ἔλυες	ἐλύετε
3	ἔλυε(ν)	ἔλυον

Here we have augment, the present stem, the connecting vowel ο/ε, and the secondary active endings, -ν, -ς, --, -μεν, -τε, -ν.

The augment occurs in the indicative mood of the secondary, or past, tenses (the imperfect, the aorist and the pluperfect). When the verb starts with a consonant, the augment is an ἐ right in front of it. When the verb starts with a vowel, the augment lengthens the vowel. α becomes η; ε becomes η; ο becomes ω. η, ι, υ, and ω are not changed when augmented. Sometimes the diphthongs, which are already long, remain unchanged, but αι usually becomes η; and ευ sometimes becomes ηυ; ει, η; and αυ, ηυ.

In augmenting a compound verb, the augment is attached to the verb stem rather than to the prepositional prefix. It is necessary, first, to take away the preposition; second, to augment the verb stem; then, third, to put the preposition back in front of the augmented stem. In the third stage it may be necessary to change the form of the preposition to make it conform to the augmented form of the verb stem. For example, the verb ἀπολύω becomes ἀπέλυον in the imperfect. The ἀπο- is first

67

taken away. -λυ- is augmented to -ελυ-. Then the preposition is put back; but its final vowel is dropped before the vowel of the augmented stem: ἀπελυ-.

There is a special accent rule that is applicable here: in compound verbs, the accent can never go back beyond the augment to the prepositional prefix. For example, ὑπῆγον is correct, not ὕπηγον. (This rule applies only to the augmented forms of the verb; the accent can often be on the preposition in unaugmented forms, such as ὕπαγε.)

Imperfect indicative middle or passive of λύω:

	Sing.	Plur.
1	ἐλυόμην	ἐλυόμεθα
2	ἐλύου	ἐλύεσθε
3	ἐλύετο	ἐλύοντο

These forms are made up just as the active ones, except that the secondary middle or passive endings are used: -μην, -σο, -το, -μεθα, -σθε, -ντο. There is contraction in the second person singular; the σ drops out, and the ε and the ο contract to ου.

The imperfect tense has no moods other than the indicative. The reason for this fact will become clear when we come to the section on the meaning of the tenses.

The Present System of Contract Verbs
-εω, -αω, and -οω

There are three types of contract verbs that show peculiarities in their paradigms in the first principal part. The stem of the verb ends in a vowel, and the vowel is contracted with the connecting vowel and ending. This creates problems both in the spelling and in the accent of the contracted forms.

The uncontracted forms never occur, though there is good reason for learning the uncontracted form of each of these verbs in the first person singular. We never see ποιέω, but if we learned only ποιῶ we would not be able to go further with the conjugation, not knowing whether the -ῶ was a contraction of -έω, -άω or -όω.

We might try to solve the problem of the spelling of the contract verbs by learning tables of contractions, but that is quite a task, and there are always certain exceptions to such rules. The student can get a fairly accurate idea of what the contracted spelling should be if he will pronounce the two contracting syllables rather rapidly. While it is difficult to be able to write out perfectly all the paradigms for the three types of contract verbs, it is much easier to recognize the forms when they occur in the Greek, and that is the most important thing.

The problem of accent may be handled thus. First, place the regular, recessive verb accent on the hypothetical uncontracted form. Second, make the proper contraction. If the accent was on a syllable that did not enter into the contraction, leave the accent as it was on the uncontracted form. If there was any kind of accent on the first one of the contracting syllables, put a circumflex upon the contracted syllable; e.g., the uncontracted ποιέομεν becomes ποιοῦμεν. If the accent was on the second of the contracting syllables, keep the same accent on the contracted syllable; e.g., the uncontracted ποιεόμεθα becomes ποιούμεθα. Unfortunately there is no shorter cut to the problem of the accent of contract verbs.

The hypothetical uncontracted forms of the contract verbs would be conjugated exactly like λύω; e.g. ἀγαπάω, ἀγαπάεις, ἀγαπάει etc. But as they never occur, and as they can be so easily ascertained, we shall give only the contracted forms that do occur.

Present indicative active:

	ποιέω	τιμάω	δηλόω
1 S	ποιῶ	τιμῶ	δηλῶ
2 S	ποιεῖς	τιμᾷς	δηλοῖς
3 S	ποιεῖ	τιμᾷ	δηλοῖ
1 P	ποιοῦμεν	τιμῶμεν	δηλοῦμεν
2 P	ποιεῖτε	τιμᾶτε	δηλοῦτε
3 P	ποιοῦσι(ν)	τιμῶσι(ν)	δηλοῦσι(ν)

69

Present indicative middle or passive:

1 S	ποιοῦμαι	τιμῶμαι	δηλοῦμαι
2 S	ποιῇ	τιμᾷ (or -ᾶσαι)	δηλοῖ
3 S	ποιεῖται	τιμᾶται	δηλοῦται
1 P	ποιούμεθα	τιμώμεθα	δηλούμεθα
2 P	ποιεῖσθε	τιμᾶσθε	δηλοῦσθε
3 P	ποιοῦνται	τιμῶνται	δηλοῦνται

Present subjunctive active:

1 S	ποιῶ	τιμῶ	δηλῶ
2 S	ποιῇς	τιμᾷς	δηλοῖς
3 S	ποιῇ	τιμᾷ	δηλοῖ
1 P	ποιῶμεν	τιμῶμεν	δηλοῦμεν
2 P	ποιῆτε	τιμᾶτε	δηλοῦτε
3 P	ποιῶσι(ν)	τιμῶσι(ν)	δηλοῦσι(ν)

Present subjunctive middle or passive:

1 S	ποιῶμαι	τιμῶμαι	δηλῶμαι
2 S	ποιῇ	τιμᾷ	δηλοῖ
3 S	ποιῆται	τιμᾶται	δηλῶται
1 P	ποιώμεθα	τιμώμεθα	δηλώμεθα
2 P	ποιῆσθε	τιμᾶσθε	δηλῶσθε
3 P	ποιῶνται	τιμῶνται	δηλῶνται

The optative mood of contract verbs is not found in the New Testament.

Present imperative active:

2 S	ποίει	τίμα	δήλου
3 S	ποιείτω	τιμάτω	δηλούτω
2 P	ποιεῖτε	τιμᾶτε	δηλοῦτε
3 P	ποιείτωσαν	τιμάτωσαν	δηλούτωσαν

Present imperative middle or passive:

2 S	ποιοῦ	τιμῶ	δηλοῦ
3 S	ποιείσθω	τιμάσθω	δηλούσθω
2 P	ποιεῖσθε	τιμᾶσθε	δηλοῦσθε
3 P	ποιείσθωσαν	τιμάσθωσαν	δηλούσθωσαν

Infinitive:

Act.	ποιεῖν	τιμᾶν	δηλοῦν
M/P	ποιεῖσθαι	τιμᾶσθαι	δηλοῦσθαι

Participle:

Act.	ποιῶν, -οῦσα, -οῦν	τιμῶν, -ῶσα, -ῶν	δηλῶν, -οῦσα, -οῦν
M/P	ποιούμενος, -η, -ον	τιμώμενος, -η, -ον	δηλούμενος, -η, -ον

Imperfect indicative active:

1 S	ἐποίουν	ἐτίμων	ἐδήλουν
2 S	ἐποίεις	ἐτίμας	ἐδήλους
3 S	ἐποίει	ἐτίμα	ἐδήλου
1 P	ἐποιοῦμεν	ἐτιμῶμεν	ἐδηλοῦμεν
2 P	ἐποιεῖτε	ἐτιμᾶτε	ἐδηλοῦτε
3 P	ἐποίουν	ἐτίμων	ἐδήλουν

Imperfect indicative middle or passive:

1 S	ἐποιούμην	ἐτιμώμην	ἐδηλούμην
2 S	ἐποιοῦ	ἐτιμῶ	ἐδηλοῦ
3 S	ἐποιεῖτο	ἐτιμᾶτο	ἐδηλοῦτο
1 P	ἐποιούμεθα	ἐτιμώμεθα	ἐδηλούμεθα
2 P	ἐποιεῖσθε	ἐτιμᾶσθε	ἐδηλοῦσθε
3 P	ἐποιοῦντο	ἐτιμῶντο	ἐδηλοῦντο

Irregularities in contract verbs: From time to time irregular contractions will be found. For example, ζάω in the indicative uses the forms that are regular for the subjunctive: ζῶ, ζῇς, ζῇ, etc.; the -οω and -αω verbs use for the subjunctive the regular indicative forms. The student should allow the context to determine the form even if it does not fit exactly into the regular paradigm.

-Μι Verbs

Historically, the -μι verbs were the earliest in use in the Greek language, before much regularity was developed. No two of the -μι verbs seem to act just alike. We shall give paradigms of some of the most common, typical -μι verbs;

71

from these the student can recognize the more unusual forms as they occur in his reading, even though he may not be able to write out complete paradigms of each verb.

Because of the irregularities of the -μι verbs, the *koine* period made -ω verbs out of some of the older -μι verbs. For example, from ἵστημι came the verbs στήκω and ἱστάνω (conjugated like λύω) and ἱστάω (conjugated like τιμάω). But the older -μι forms have continued in use, so the student of the New Testament has to deal with both of them.

Regularly the -μι verb does not have the thematic, or connecting, vowel that is typical of the -ω verb, so it is also called the athematic or nonthematic verb. The endings are added directly to the stem of the verb, which always ends in a vowel. And the student will notice that that vowel is quite fluid; usually the long form of the vowel is used in the singular and the short form in the plural.

Present indicative active of ἵστημι:

	Sing.	Plur.
1	ἵστημι	ἵσταμεν
2	ἵστης	ἵστατε
3	ἵστησι(ν)	ἱστᾶσι(ν)

Here we see the -μι set of endings (-μι, -ς, -σι, -μεν, -τε and -σι or -ασι) added to the present stem, which uses the long η in the singular and α in the plural.

Present indicative middle or passive of ἵστημι:

	Sing.	Plur.
1	ἵσταμαι	ἱστάμεθα
2	ἵστασαι	ἵστασθε
3	ἵσταται	ἵστανται

Here we see the regular primary middle/passive endings added to the short form of the present stem (notice the absence of contraction in the second person singular).

72

Present subjunctive active of ἵστημι:

	Sing.	Plur.
1	ἱστῶ	ἱστῶμεν
2	ἱστῇς	ἱστῆτε
3	ἱστῇ	ἱστῶσι(ν)

Present subjunctive middle or passive of ἵστημι:

	Sing.	Plur.
1	ἱστῶμαι	ἱστώμεθα
2	ἱστῇ	ἱστῆσθε
3	ἱστῆται	ἱστῶνται

The present optative does not occur in the New Testament.

Present active imperative of ἵστημι:

	Sing.	Plur.
2	ἵστη	ἵστατε
3	ἱστάτω	ἱστάτωσαν

Present imperative middle or passive of ἵστημι:

	Sing.	Plur.
2	ἵστασο	ἵστασθε
3	ἱστάσθω	ἱστάσθωσαν

Present infinitives of ἵστημι:

Active: ἱστάναι   Middle/passive: ἵστασθαι

Present active participle of ἵστημι:

	Masc.	Fem.	Neut.
		Sing.	
N.V.	ἱστάς	ἱστᾶσα	ἱστάν
Gen.	ἱστάντος	ἱστάσης	ἱστάντος
Dat.	ἱστάντι	ἱστάσῃ	ἱστάντι
Acc.	ἱστάντα	ἱστᾶσαν	ἱστάν

73

Plur.

N.V.	ἱστάντες	ἱστᾶσαι	ἱστάντα
Gen.	ἱστάντων	ἱστασῶν	ἱστάντων
Dat.	ἱστᾶσι(ν)	ἱστάσαις	ἱστᾶσι(ν)
Acc.	ἱστάντας	ἱστάσας	ἱστάντα

Present middle or passive participle of ἵστημι: ἱστάμενος, -η, -ον (declined like ἀγαθός, -η, -ον).

Imperfect indicative active of ἵστημι:

	Sing.	Plur.
1	ἵστην	ἵσταμεν
2	ἵστης	ἵστατε
3	ἵστη	ἵστασαν

Imperfect indicative middle or passive of ἵστημι:

	Sing.	Plur.
1	ἱστάμην	ἱστάμεθα
2	ἵστασο	ἵστασθε
3	ἵστατο	ἵσταντο

Τίθημι

τίθημι has as its short form of the present stem τιθε-, so the following differences from ἵστημι should be noted:

Present indicative active plural: τίθεμεν, τίθετε, τιθέασι(ν).
Present indicative middle or passive: τίθεμαι, τίθεσαι, etc.
Present optative does not occur in the N.T.
Present active imperative: τίθει, τιθέτω, etc.
Present middle/passive imperative: τίθεσο, τιθέσθω, etc.
Present infinitives: act., τιθέναι; m/p, τίθεσθαι.

Present active participle of τίθημι:

	Masc.	Fem.	Neut.
		Sing.	
N.V.	τιθείς	τιθεῖσα	τιθέν
Gen.	τιθέντος	τιθείσης	τιθέντος
Dat.	τιθέντι	τιθείσῃ	τιθέντι
Acc.	τιθέντα	τιθεῖσαν	τιθέν

Plur.

N.V.	τιθέντες	τιθεῖσαι	τιθέντα
Gen.	τιθέντων	τιθεισῶν	τιθέντων
Dat.	τιθεῖσι(ν)	τιθείσαις	τιθεῖσι(ν)
Acc.	τιθέντας	τιθείσας	τιθέντα

Present middle or passive participle: τιθέμενος, -η, -ον.
Imperfect indicative active: ἐτίθην, ἐτίθεις, ἐτίθει, ἐτίθεμεν, ἐτίθετε, ἐτίθεσαν.
Imperfect indicative middle or passive: ἐτιθέμην, ἐτίθεσο, etc.

Δίδωμι

δίδωμι has as its short form of the root διδο-, so the following differences from ἵστημι, should be noted:
Present indicative active plural: δίδομεν, δίδοτε, διδόασι(ν).
Present indicative middle or passive: δίδομαι, δίδοσαι, etc.
Present optative does not occur in the N.T.
Present active imperative: δίδου, διδότω, etc.
Present m/p imperative: δίδοσο, διδόσθω, etc.
Present infinitives: act., διδόναι; m/p δίδοσθαι.

Present active participle:

	Masc.	Fem.	Neut.
		Sing.	
N.V.	διδούς	διδοῦσα	διδόν
Gen.	διδόντος	διδούσης	διδόντος
Dat.	διδόντι	διδούσῃ	διδόντι
Acc.	διδόντα	διδοῦσαν	διδόν

		Plur.	
N.V.	διδόντες	διδοῦσαι	διδόντα
Gen.	διδόντων	διδουσῶν	διδόντων
Dat.	διδοῦσι(ν)	διδούσαις	διδοῦσι(ν)
Acc.	διδόντας	διδούσας	διδόντα

Present m/p participle: διδόμενος, -η, -ον.

Imperfect active indicative: ἐδίδουν, ἐδίδους, ἐδίδου, ἐδίδομεν, ἐδίδοτε, ἐδίδοσαν.

Imperfect m/p indicative: ἐδιδόμην, ἐδίδοσο, etc.

Δείκνυμι

δείκνυμι uses the stem δεικνυ- throughout, so the following differences from ἵστημι should be noted:

Present indicative plural: δείκνυμεν, δείκνντε, δεικνύασι(ν).

Present active imperative: δείκνυ, δεικνύτω, etc.

Present m/p imperative: δείκνυσο, δεικνύσθω, etc.

Present infinitives: act., δεικνύναι; m/p δείκνυσθαι.

Present active participle: δεικνύς, δεικνῦσα, δεικνύν (genitives: δεικνύντος, δεικνύσης, δεικνύντος, etc.)

Present m/p participle: δεικνύμενος, -η, -ον.

Imperfect indicative active: ἔδεικνυν, ἔδεικνυς, etc.

Imperfect indicative m/p: ἐδεικνύμην, etc.

As δεικνύω is in common use in the *koine*, many of its forms, as regular -ω verbs, are used instead of the -μι forms.

Εἰμί

As in most languages, the verb "to be" is most irregular in Greek.

Present indicative active of εἰμί:

	Sing.	Plur.
1	εἰμί	ἐσμέν
2	εἶ	ἐστέ
3	ἐστί(ν)	εἰσί(ν)

All of these forms except εἶ are enclitics unless emphasis is desired.

Naturally, no middle or passive forms are used.

Present subjunctive active of εἰμί:

	Sing.	Plur.
1	ὦ	ὦμεν
2	ᾖς	ἦτε
3	ᾖ	ὦσι(ν)

Present optative active of εἰμί:

	Sing.	Plur.
1	εἴην	εἴημεν
2	εἴης	εἴητε
3	εἴη	εἴησαν

Present active imperative of εἰμί:

	Sing.	Plur.
2	ἴσθι	ἔστε
3	ἔστω (or ἤτω)	ἔστωσαν

Present active infinitive: εἶναι.

Present active participle: ὤν, οὖσα, ὄν (declined like λύων, λύουσα, λῦον).

Imperfect indicative active of εἰμί:

	Sing.	Plur.
1	ἦν (or ἤμην)	ἦμεν (or ἤμεθα)
2	ἦς (or ἦσθα)	ἦτε
3	ἦν	ἦσαν

When the middle or passive endings are used, there is no difference in meaning.

The verb εἰμί should not be confused with the verb εἶμι, a very irregular future meaning "I shall go."

Φημί

φημί, "say," has a few forms in use:

Present indicative active of φημί:

	Sing.	Plur.
1	φημί	φαμέν
2	φής	φατέ
3	φησί(ν)	φασί(ν)

Imperfect indicative active of φημί:

	Sing.	Plur.
1	ἔφην	ἔφαμεν
2	ἔφης	ἔφατε
3	ἔφη	ἔφασαν

77

Some Additions to the Root to Form the Present Stem

The present stem of the verb may be found by dropping the -ω, -μι, -ομαι, or -μαι from the first principal part. But the root of the verb may be different from the present stem. The root can be seen more easily in the other principal parts; usually it can be easily found by dropping -σω from the second principal part.

All the dictionaries give the verbs arranged alphabetically according to the first principal part. When the student wants to look up a word which he has found in the present or imperfect, he can easily discover the present stem, add an -ω or -μι (-ομαι or -μαι| for deponents), and look up that form in the dictionary.

If, however, he is working with a form built from one of the other principal parts, he can discover the root of the verb (or at least one form of the root) by dropping the various signs and endings that make the form what it is. The root may be the same as the present stem, and he can add the present ending and look it up. But quite often he will not find the verb, because the root is often "dressed up" in various ways to make the present stem. The student will find it most helpful if he remembers at least some of the most common prefixes and infixes that are used to form the present stem from the root. With very few exceptions these additions will appear only in the first principal part.

σσ or ττ verbs: The σσ is more commonly found in the *koine* period, whereas the ττ was common in the Attic Classical period; e.g., πράσσω (πράττω) from the root πραγ-, which is seen, sometimes slightly camouflaged, in the other principal parts and in various nouns.

Nasal infixes: μ or ν is inserted, with or without an accompanying vowel, one or more times in the root. σκληρύνω from the root σκληρ-. λαμβάνω from the root λαβ-. Sometimes these present tense "trimmings" are found in some of the other principal parts where they really do not belong; e.g., the *koine* future of λαμβάνω is λήμψομαι, whereas it was λήψομαι in the Classical period.

σκ or ισκ verbs: εὑρίσκω from the root εὑρ- or εὑρη-.

Reduplicated verbs: δίδωμι from the root δω- or δο-. τίθημι from the root θη- or θε-. This reduplication should not be confused with that found in the perfect tenses. This present tense reduplication uses the vowel iota, while the perfect uses epsilon.

Y class verbs: A y sound is added to the root in various ways. πικραίνω from the root πικραν- shows the addition of an iota. ἀγγέλλω from the root ἀγγελ- shows the sound brought out by the second lambda.

Sometimes several of these may be combined in one verb; e.g., μιμνήσκω from the root μνη-.

-εω, -αω, and -οω verbs: These are somewhat different from this category. In the present system we are bothered with the contractions of the ε, α and o. But in the other principal parts the contract verbs are most regular. The ε and the α lengthen to η, and the o lengthens to ω; then they run almost as regularly as λύω: ποιέω, ποιήσω, etc.; τιμάω, τιμήσω,, etc.; and δικαιόω, δικαιώσω, etc. In looking up one of these words, the student should drop an η back to ε or α, and an ω back to o when he is dealing with a form based on any principal part other than the first.

Section 2

The Second Principal Part

Under the second principal part are found the future active and the future middle (the future passive comes under the sixth principal part).

Theoretically, the future tense should have only the indicative mood, but actually it has infinitives and participles that are used for indicatives in certain constructions.

Future indicative active of λύω (Sigmatic Future):

	Sing.	Plur.
1	λύσω	λύσομεν
2	λύσεις	λύσετε
3	λύσει	λύσουσι(ν)

Future indicative middle of λύω:

	Sing.	Plur.
1	λύσομαι	λυσόμεθα
2	λύσῃ	λύσεσθε
3	λύσεται	λύσονται

Future active infinitive: λύσειν

Future middle infinitive: λύσεσθαι

Future active participle: λύσων, λύσουσα, λῦσον, declined like λύων, λύουσα, λῦον.

Future middle participle: λυσόμενος, -η, -ον, declined like ἀγαθός, -η, -ον.

It will be noted that these forms have exactly the same endings as the corresponding present forms, but a σ has been added just before the connecting vowel and ending. This σ is added to the root of the verb, which may or may not be the same as the present stem (remember the various ways of "dressing up" roots to make present stems).

When the σ is added to a root ending in π, β or φ the two are written ψ; e.g., βλέψω is the future of βλέπω.

When the σ is added to κ, γ or χ the two become ξ; e.g., κηρύξω from the root κηρυγ-.

When the σ is added to a root ending in τ, δ or θ, those letters are dropped and only the σ remains.

With the exception of the verbs showing these changes made for the sake of euphony, the sigmatic future forms are very easy to handle; remember to look for the significant sign σ and the endings found in the present.

The Liquid Future: Ἀγγελῶ

Roots ending in one of the liquids (λ, μ, ν, ρ) regularly have the other main type of future, the liquid future. It will be noted that it is conjugated just like the present of the -εω verb.

Future indicative active of ἀγγέλλω (root ἀγγελ-):

	Sing.	Plur.
1	ἀγγελῶ	ἀγγελοῦμεν
2	ἀγγελεῖς	ἀγγελεῖτε
3	ἀγγελεῖ	ἀγγελοῦσι(ν)

Future indicative middle:

	Sing.	Plur.
1	ἀγγελοῦμαι	ἀγγελούμεθα
2	ἀγγελῇ	ἀγγελεῖσθε
3	ἀγγελεῖται	ἀγγελοῦνται

Future infinitive active: ἀγγελεῖν.

Future infinitive middle: ἀγγελεῖσθαι.

Future participle active: ἀγγελῶν, -οῦσα, -οῦν.

Future participle middle: ἀγγελούμενος, -η, -ον.

Futures Conjugated Like Presents

A very few verbs have futures that belong to neither of these two regular classes. They are handled just like presents, but they are different from the first principal part. ἐσθίω has for its future φάγομαι; πίνω has πίομαι; εἶμι, "I shall go," has no other forms than the future; except for the accent it is conjugated like the present εἰμί.

Section 3

The Third Principal Part

Under the third principal part are found the aorist active and middle (the aorist passive comes under the sixth).

81

There are six different kinds of aorists under this principa part: three first aorists, two second aorists, and the mixed aorist.

I a: The Sigmatic First Aorist —῎Ελυσα:

Aorist indicative active:

	Sing.	Plur.
1	ἔλυσα	ἐλύσαμεν
2	ἔλυσας	ἐλύσατε
3	ἔλυσε(ν)	ἔλυσαν

Note the significant features:

a. Augment (only in the indicative mood), acting exactly like the augment of the imperfect. See page 67.

b. The root of the verb, which may or may not be the same as the present stem.

c. The sign σ, which is joined to the root like the σ of the future; e.g., π and σ will be written ψ. See page 80.

d. The connecting vowel α, except in the third person singular, where it is ε.

e. A slight variation of the secondary active endings: --, ς, --, μεν, τε, ν, the same as those used in the imperfect except for the first person singular.

Aorist indicative middle:

	Sing.	Plur.
1	ἐλυσάμην	ἐλυσάμεθα
2	ἐλύσω	ἐλύσασθε
3	ἐλύσατο	ἐλύσαντο

Here we have the same augment, root, sign σ, and the connecting vowel α, which does not become ε in the third person singular. The endings, though, are the secondary middle endings, μην, σο, το, μεθα, σθε, ντο. In the second person singular there has been a contraction, ἐλύσασο becoming ἐλύσω.

Aorist subjunctive active:

	Sing.	Plur.
1	λύσω	λύσωμεν
2	λύσῃς	λύσητε
3	λύσῃ	λύσωσι(ν)

a. There is no augment in any mood except the indicative, so to form the other moods the augment must be dropped from the third principal part.

b. The root of the verb.

c. The sign σ.

d. The long connecting vowel ω/η.

e. The primary active endings. As in the present, the elements d and e come together in the singular, but they are easily separated in the plural.

Aorist subjunctive middle:

	Sing.	Plur.
1	λύσωμαι	λυσώμεθα
2	λύσῃ	λύσησθε
3	λύσηται	λύσωνται

This is the same as the active except that the primary middle endings are used: μαι, σαι (here, as often, contracted), ται, μεθα, σθε, νται.

Aorist optative active:

	Sing.	Plur.
1	λύσαιμι	λύσαιμεν
2	λύσαις	λύσαιτε
3	λύσαι	λύσαιεν

Here we see the root, the sign σ, the connecting vowel αι, and an adaptation of the secondary active endings. The optative occurs so seldom that the student does not need to spend much time trying to master it; he can usually spot optative forms by the connecting vowel being a diphthong with an iota in it.

83

Aorist optative middle:

	Sing.	Plur.
1	λυσαίμην	λυσαίμεθα
2	λύσαιο	λύσαισθε
3	λύσαιτο	λύσαιντο

This is the same as the active except for the secondary middle endings.

Aorist imperative active:

	Sing.	Plur.
2	λῦσον	λύσατε
3	λυσάτω	λυσάτωσαν

Aorist imperative middle:

	Sing.	Plur.
2	λῦσαι	λύσασθε
3	λυσάσθω	λυσάσθωσαν

We can see the significant aorist signs through λυσα-. The endings are much the same as those we saw in the present.

Aorist infinitive active: λῦσαι.

Aorist infinitive middle: λύσασθαι.

(In the active, the accent is not recessive but always is on the penult; e.g., βαπτῖσαι, not βάπτισαι.)

Aorist participle active:

	Masc.	Fem.	Neut.
		Sing.	
N.V.	λύσας	λύσασα	λῦσαν
Gen.	λύσαντος	λυσάσης	λύσαντος
Dat.	λύσαντι	λυσάσῃ	λύσαντι
Acc.	λύσαντα	λύσασαν	λῦσαν

Plur.

N.V.	λύσαντες	λύσασαι	λύσαντα
Gen.	λυσάντων	λυσασῶν	λυσάντων
Dat.	λύσασι(ν)	λυσάσαις	λύσασι(ν)
Acc.	λύσαντας	λυσάσας	λύσαντα

The masculine and neuter are declined in the third declension, while the feminine is first declension like δόξα.

Aorist middle participle: λυσάμενος, -η, -ον, declined like ἀγαθός, -η, -ον.

I b: The Liquid First Aorist —Ἥγγειλα (from ἀγγέλλω)

Aorist indicative active:

	Sing.	Plur.
1	ἤγγειλα	ἠγγείλαμεν
2	ἤγγειλας	ἠγγείλατε
3	ἤγγειλε(ν)	ἤγγειλαν

The distinguishing signs of the liquid aorist are:

a. Augment (in the indicative mood only).

b. The root of the verb, which must end in a liquid *(λ, μ, ν, ρ)*, and which is often lengthened (here, for example, ε is lengthened to ει).

c. The connecting vowel α (ε in the third singular active).

d. The secondary active endings, --, ς, --, μεν, τε, ν.

Aorist indicative middle:

	Sing.	Plur.
1	ἠγγειλάμην	ἠγγειλάμεθα
2	ἠγγείλω	ἠγγείλασθε
3	ἠγγείλατο	ἠγγείλαντο

This is the same as the active except that the middle endings are used, with contraction, as usual, in the second person singular.

Aorist subjunctive active:

	Sing.	Plur.
1	ἀγγείλω	ἀγγείλωμεν
2	ἀγγείλῃς	ἀγγείλητε
3	ἀγγείλῃ	ἀγγείλωσι(ν)

We have given enough of the liquid aorist to show that the endings are just the same as the sigmatic first aorist. All the other forms can be easily made by putting ἀγγειλ- in place of λυσ- in the paradigms of the sigmatic aorist.

I c: The Ka First Aorist—Ἔθηκα (from Τίθημι)

Aorist indicative active:

	Sing.	Plur.
1	ἔθηκα	ἐθήκαμεν
2	ἔθηκας	ἐθήκατε
3	ἔθηκε(ν)	ἔθηκαν

This is just like the sigmatic aorist except that it has a κ in place of a σ as its significant sign. This aorist occurs in only a very few verbs, and only in the aorist indicative active. All the other forms of such verbs are conjugated as root second aorists.

II a: The Regular (or Thematic) Second Aorist--

Ἔλιπον (from Λείπω)

	Sing.	Plur.
1	ἔλιπον	ἐλίπομεν
2	ἔλιπες	ἐλίπετε
3	ἔλιπε(ν)	ἔλιπον

This is made up of the following elements:

a. Augment (in the indicative mood only).

b. The root of the verb, which in these verbs is different from the present stem, usually shorter; e.g., λιπ instead of λειπ.

c. The connecting vowel o/ε.

d. The secondary active endings ν, ς, --, $\mu\varepsilon\nu$, $\tau\varepsilon$, ν.

It will be noted that elements a, c, and d are just like the imperfect; the difference is in element b, where the imperfect uses the present stem.

Aorist indicative middle:

	Sing.	Plur.
1	ἐλιπόμην	ἐλιπόμεθα
2	ἐλίπου	ἐλίπεσθε
3	ἐλίπετο	ἐλίποντο

This is the same as the active except for the middle endings, and the same as the imperfect indicative middle except for the root instead of the present stem.

Aorist subjunctive active:

	Sing.	Plur.
1	λίπω	λίπωμεν
2	λίπῃς	λίπητε
3	λίπῃ	λίπωσι(ν)

We see no augment, of course; the root of the verb; and the same combination of the long connecting vowel ω/η and the endings as in the present active subjunctive.

Aorist subjunctive middle:

	Sing.	Plur.
1	λίπωμαι	λιπώμεθα
2	λίπῃ	λίπησθε
3	λίπηται	λίπωνται

This is the same as the active except for the middle endings.

Aorist optative active:

	Sing.	Plur.
1	λίποιμι	λίποιμεν
2	λίποις	λίποιτε
3	λίποι	λίποιεν

Aorist optative middle:

	Sing.	Plur.
1	λιποίμην	λιποίμεθα
2	λίποιο	λίποισθε
3	λίποιτο	λίποιντο

This is the same as the present optative except for the use of the root instead of the present stem. Note the significant connecting vowel *οι*.

Aorist imperative active:

	Sing.	Plur.
2	λίπε	λίπετε
3	λιπέτω	λιπέτωσαν

Aorist imperative middle:

	Sing.	Plur.
2	λιποῦ	λίπεσθε
3	λιπέσθω	λιπέσθωσαν

These imperatives are the same as the present except for the use of the root instead of the present stem.

Aorist infinitive active:

λιπεῖν (with the circumflex accent always on the ultima).

Aorist infinitive middle:

λιπέσθαι (with the acute accent always on the penult).

Aorist participle active:

λιπών, -ουσα, -ον, declined like λύων, -ουσα, -ον (but notice that the accent here is not recessive).

Aorist participle middle:

λιπόμενος, -η, -ον, declined like ἀγαθός, -η, -ον.

II b: The Root (or Non-thematic) Second Aorist-- ἔστην (from ἵστημι)

Aorist indicative active:

	Sing.	Plur.
1	ἔστην	ἔστημεν
2	ἔστης	ἔστητε
3	ἔστη	ἔστησαν

The elements of this aorist are:

a. Augment (in the indicative mood only).

b. The root of the verb, which must end in a vowel. Often a short form of the root vowel will be used in the plural.

c. The secondary endings, ν, ς, --, μεν, τε, σαν.

This differs from the regular second aorist in having no connecting, or thematic, vowel, and in using an alternate ending in the third person plural.

Aorist indicative middle—ἐδόμην (from δίδωμι):

	Sing.	Plur.
1	ἐδόμην	ἐδόμεθα
2	ἔδου	ἔδοσθε
3	ἔδοτο	ἔδοντο

This is formed just like the active, except that the middle secondary endings are used.

Aorist subjunctive active--στῶ (from ἵστημι):

	Sing.	Plur.
1	στῶ	στῶμεν
2	στῇς	στῆτε
3	στῇ	στῶσι(ν)

Aorist subjunctive middle--θῶμαι (from τίθημι):

	Sing.	Plur.
1	θῶμαι	θώμεθα
2	θῇ	θῆσθε
3	θῆται	θῶνται

89

No optative forms occur in the New Testament.

Aorist imperative active and middle: The forms are regularly made by adding the imperative endings, active and middle, to the long or short form of the root. There is some variation in the second person singular active; e.g., στά or στῆθι.

Aorist infinitive active: στῆναι (with the accent on the penult).

Aorist infinitive middle: θέσθαι (from the verb τίθημι).

Aorist participle active: στάς, στᾶσα, στάν, declined like λύσας, λύσασα, λύσαν.

Aorist participle middle: The middle ending -μενος, -η, -ον, is added to the long or short form of the root and is declined like ἀγαθός, η, ον; e.g., θέμενος from τίθημι.

III: The Mixed Aorist—Ἔλιπα (from λείπω):

In the *koine* period, sometimes the first aorist connecting vowel and endings were placed on second aorist stems, making forms like: ἔλιπα, ἔλιπας, ἐλίπαμεν, ἐλίπατε, ἔλιπαν. These mixed forms show up only in the aorist indicative active and can be easily identified when they occur.

Section 4

The Fourth Principal Part

Under the fourth principal part is found the perfect system (perfect, pluperfect, and future perfect) in the active voice.

The First Perfect System
Λέλυκα from Λύω

Perfect indicative active:

	Sing.	Plur.
1	λέλυκα	λελύκαμεν
2	λέλυκας	λελύκατε
3	λέλυκε(ν)	λελύκασι(ν)

90

These forms are made up as follows:

a. Reduplication: With verbs starting with a consonant, the reduplication is made by using the initial consonant and adding the vowel ε; e.g., for the verb λύω the reduplication is λε-. With verbs starting with a vowel, the vowel is lengthened (so the reduplication will appear just the same as augment). If a verb begins with more than one consonant, usually only the first consonant is used with the ε; at times the ε is used without any consonant. Verbs starting with sigma regularly have ἑ as reduplication.

b. The root (or one form of the root) of the verb (λυ- from λύω).

c. κ, the sign of the first perfect (the second perfect will not have this).

d. The connecting vowel α (ε in the third person sing.)

e. A form of the primary personal endings: --, ς, --, μεν, τε, σι.

Perfect subjunctive active:

	Sing.	Plur.
1	λελύκω	λελύκωμεν
2	λελύκῃς	λελύκητε
3	λελύκῃ	λελύκωσι(ν)

Here we see the same reduplication, root, and sign κ. Then we see the regular subjunctive endings ω, ῃς, ῃ, ωμεν, ητε, ωσι(ν).

Usually this is formed periphrastically, using the perfect active participle and the present subjunctive of the verb εἰμί; e.g., λελυκὼς ὦ and λελυκότες ὦμεν.

No optative forms are found in the New Testament.

Perfect imperative active:

	Sing.	Plur.
2	λέλυκε	λελύκετε
3	λελυκέτω	λελυκέτωσαν

These forms are almost never used in the New Testament.
Perfect active infinitive: λελυκέναι.

Perfect active participle:

	Masc.	Fem.	Neut.
		Sing.	
N.V.	λελυκώς	λελυκυῖα	λελυκός
Gen.	λελυκότος	λελυκυίας	λελυκότος
Dat.	λελυκότι	λελυκυίᾳ	λελυκότι
Acc.	λελυκότα	λελυκυῖαν	λελυκός
		Plur.	
N.V.	λελυκότες	λελυκυῖαι	λελυκότα
Gen.	λελυκότων	λελυκυιῶν	λελυκότων
Dat.	λελυκόσι(ν)	λελυκυίαις	λελυκόσι(ν)
Acc.	λελυκότας	λελυκυίας	λελυκότα

Pluperfect active indicative:

	Sing.	Plur.
1	ἐλελύκειν	ἐλελύκειμεν
2	ἐλελύκεις	ἐλελύκειτε
3	ἐλελύκει	ἐλελύκεισαν

The pluperfect has only the indicative mood.

It has regularly augment as well as reduplication, though in the *koine* period the augment is often omitted. In verbs starting with a vowel, the augment and reduplication will be united. The connecting vowel here is ει, and the regular secondary active endings are used: ν, ς, --, μεν, τε, σαν.

Future perfect active indicative:

	Sing.	Plur.
1	λελύξω	λελύξομεν
2	λελύξεις	λελύξετε
3	λελύξει	λελύξουσι(ν)

Here we have reduplication, root, the signs of the perfect and the future (κ and ς) written together as ξ, and the connecting vowels and endings ω, εις, ει, ομεν, ετε, ουσι(ν). These forms can be made periphrastically, using the perfect active participle and the future of the verb εἰμί; e.g., λελυκὼς ἔσομαι.

Only the indicative mood occurs, and it only rarely.

The Second Perfect System

It is not necessary to give paradigms for this, as it is just the same as the first perfect except that it does not have the sign κ.

Some irregularities show in this system (e.g., the subjunctive of οἶδα is εἰδῶ), but they cannot be given in a brief grammar; the student will find these unusual forms in the lexicons.

Section 5

The Fifth Principal Part

Under this we find the perfect system (perfect, pluperfect, and future perfect) in the middle and passive voices (which have the same forms).

Perfect indicative middle or passive:

	Sing.	Plur.
1	λέλυμαι	λελύμεθα
2	λέλυσαι	λέλυσθε
3	λέλυται	λέλυνται

These forms are very simple, consisting of reduplication, the verb root, and the primary middle or passive endings, μαι, σαι, ται, μεθα, σθε, νται. When the root of the verb ends in a consonant, there may be various euphonic changes necessary to join the ending to it. The third person plural is regularly made periphrastically, using the perfect middle or passive participle and the present of the verb εἰμί.

Subjunctive and optative forms almost never occur; they are

93

formed by using the perfect middle or passive participle and the present subjunctive or optative of the verb εἰμί.

Present imperative middle or passive:

	Sing.	Plur.
2	λέλυσο	λέλυσθε
3	λελύσθω	λελύσθωσαν

Perfect participle middle or passive: λελυμένος, -η, -ον (declined like ἀγαθός, -η, -ον).

Pluperfect indicative middle or passive:

	Sing.	Plur.
1	ἐλελύμην	ἐλελύμεθα
2	ἐλέλυσο	ἐλέλυσθε
3	ἐλέλυτο	ἐλέλυντο

Here we see augment (often omitted), reduplication, the verb root, and the regular secondary middle or passive endings, μην, σο, το, μεθα, σθε, ντο. There will be euphonic changes necessary at times to add the endings to roots ending in consonants.

Future perfect indicative middle or passive: This is found in the New Testament in only a few periphrastic forms, made up of the perfect middle or passive participle of the main verb and the future indicative of the verb εἰμί: λελυμένος ἔσομαι, λελυμένοι ἐσόμεθα, etc.

Section 6

The Sixth Principal Part

Under this occur the aorist passive and the future passive.

First aorist passive indicative of λύω:

	Sing.	Plur.
1	ἐλύθην	ἐλύθημεν
2	ἐλύθης	ἐλύθητε
3	ἐλύθη	ἐλύθησαν

94

These forms are made up thus:

a. Augment (in the indicative mood only, of course).

b. The root of the verb (or one form of it).

c. The sign ϑ. (This will be absent in the second aorist passive.)

d. The connecting vowel η.

e. The secondary active personal endings: ν, ς, --, $\mu\varepsilon\nu$, $\tau\varepsilon$ and $\sigma\alpha\nu$. There is some mystery as to why active endings are used here; it is possible that this developed from the aorist active.

First aorist passive subjunctive:

	Sing.	Plur.
1	$\lambda\upsilon\vartheta\tilde{\omega}$	$\lambda\upsilon\vartheta\tilde{\omega}\mu\varepsilon\nu$
2	$\lambda\upsilon\vartheta\tilde{\eta}\varsigma$	$\lambda\upsilon\vartheta\tilde{\eta}\tau\varepsilon$
3	$\lambda\upsilon\vartheta\tilde{\eta}$	$\lambda\upsilon\vartheta\tilde{\omega}\sigma\iota(\nu)$

The active subjunctive connecting vowel and endings are contracted with the connecting vowel η.

Aorist passive optative:

	Sing.	Plur.
1	$\lambda\upsilon\vartheta\varepsilon\acute{\iota}\eta\nu$	$\lambda\upsilon\vartheta\varepsilon\acute{\iota}\eta\mu\varepsilon\nu$
2	$\lambda\upsilon\vartheta\varepsilon\acute{\iota}\eta\varsigma$	$\lambda\upsilon\vartheta\varepsilon\acute{\iota}\eta\tau\varepsilon$
3	$\lambda\upsilon\vartheta\varepsilon\acute{\iota}\eta$	$\lambda\upsilon\vartheta\varepsilon\acute{\iota}\eta\sigma\alpha\nu$

The student will recognize the few forms that occur by the sign ϑ and by remembering that the optative connecting vowel is a diphthong one letter of which is always iota.

Aorist passive imperative:

	Sing.	Plur.
2	$\lambda\acute{\upsilon}\vartheta\eta\tau\iota$	$\lambda\acute{\upsilon}\vartheta\eta\tau\varepsilon$
3	$\lambda\upsilon\vartheta\acute{\eta}\tau\omega$	$\lambda\upsilon\vartheta\acute{\eta}\tau\omega\sigma\alpha\nu$

Aorist passive infinitive: $\lambda\upsilon\vartheta\tilde{\eta}\nu\alpha\iota$.

95

Aorist passive participle:

	Masc.	Fem.	Neut.
		Sing.	
N.V.	λυθείς	λυθεῖσα	λυθέν
Gen.	λυθέντος	λυθείσης	λυθέντος
Dat.	λυθέντι	λυθείσῃ	λυθέντι
Acc.	λυθέντα	λυθεῖσαν	λυθέν
		Plur.	
N.V.	λυθέντες	λυθεῖσαι	λυθέντα
Gen.	λυθέντων	λυθεισῶν	λυθέντων
Dat.	λυθεῖσι(ν)	λυθείσαις	λυθεῖσι(ν)
Acc.	λυθέντας	λυθείσας	λυθέντα

First future passive indicative of λύω:

	Sing.	Plur.
1	λυθήσομαι	λυθησόμεθα
2	λυθήσῃ	λυθήσεσθε
3	λυθήσεται	λυθήσονται

These forms are made up thus:

a. The root of the verb.

b. The sign ϑ.

c. The vowel η.

d. The future sign σ.

e. The o/ε connecting vowel.

f. The primary passive endings, μαι, σαι (contracted as usual), ται, μεθα, σϑε, νται.

With so many marks of identification, these forms are very easy to recognize.

Future passive infinitive: λυθήσεσθαι.

Future passive participle: λυθησόμενος, -η, -ον, declined like ἀγαθός, -η, -ον. (Only one occurs in the N.T.: Hebrews 3:5).

The second aorist and future passive: These are just the same as the first aorist and future passive except that they do not contain the sign ϑ. No new paradigms are needed.

Section 7

Principal Parts of Irregular Verbs

We shall give a representative list of some of the most common and typical of the irregular verbs. It will be most helpful to the student if he will memorize all, or at least a goodly number, of these. When he knows the principal parts of a verb he can know which paradigms to use and how to derive from them any form of the verb. If, for example, the student knows just the first form, he may not be able to go beyond the present system; ἀγγέλλω is a good case of that. But when he knows the second principal part as ἀγγελῶ, he has his starting point for the future active and middle and knows that he must use the paradigm for the liquid future. ἤγγειλα leads him to the liquid aorist. ἤγγελκα is the first perfect. ἤγγελμαι gives the start for the perfect middle or passive. ἠγγέλην shows that he must use the second aorist and future passive forms.

Also when a student knows the principal parts of a verb and comes across a form made under one of the later parts, he will be able to remember the first principal part, the form that is presented in alphabetical order in the lexicon.

The forms in parentheses do not occur in the New Testament but are found elsewhere in the language; it is probably easier to remember them than to remember to leave them out.

1. ἀγγέλλω (announce), ἀγγελῶ, ἤγγειλα, (ἤγγελκα), ἤγγελμαι, ἠγγέλην.

2. ἄγω (lead), ἄξω, ἤγαγον or ἦξα, (ἦχα), ἦγμαι, ἤχθην.

3. αἱρέω (take), αἱρήσομαι or ἑλῶ, εἷλον, (ἥρηκα), ᾕρημαι, ᾑρέθην.

4. αἴρω (raise), ἀρῶ, ἦρα, ἦρκα, ἦρμαι, ἤρθην.

5. ἀκούω (hear), ἀκούσω, ἤκουσα, ἀκήκοα, ἤκουσμαι, ἠκούσθην.

6. ἁμαρτάνω (sin), ἁμαρτήσω, ἥμαρτον or ἡμάρτησα, ἡμάρτηκα, --, --.

7. ἀνοίγω (open), ἀνοίξω, ἠνέῳξα, ἠνέῳγα, ἠνέῳγμαι, ἠνεῴχθην (the last four parts can also begin ἀνεῳ-, ἀνῳ-, ἠνῳ-, or ἠνοι-).

97

8. ἀρέσκω (please), ἀρέσω, ἤρεσα, --, --, --.

9. βαίνω (go), βήσομαι, ἔβην, βέβηκα, --, --.

10. βάλλω (throw), βαλῶ, ἔβαλον, βέβληκα, βέβλημαι, ἐβλήθην.

11. γίνομαι (become), γενήσομαι, ἐγενόμην, γέγονα, γεγένημαι, ἐγενήθην.

12. γινώσκω (know), γνώσομαι, ἔγνων, ἔγνωκα, ἔγνωσμαι, ἐγνώσθην.

13. γράφω (write), γράψω, ἔγραψα, γέγραφα, γέγραμμαι, ἐγράφην.

14. δείκνυμι (show), δείξω, ἔδειξα, (δέδειχα), δέδειγμαι, ἐδείχθην.

15. δέω (bind), δήσω, ἔδησα, δέδεχα, δέδεμαι, ἐδέθην.

16. δίδωμι (give), δώσω, ἔδωκα, δέδωκα, δέδομαι, ἐδόθην.

17. δύναμαι (can), δυνήσομαι, --, --, --, ἠδυνήθην or ἠδυνάσθην (imperfect ἐδυνάμην or ἠδυνάμην).

18. ἐγείρω (raise), ἐγερῶ, ἤγειρα, --, ἐγήγερμαι, ἠγέρθην.

19. ἐλπίζω (hope), ἐλπιῶ, ἤλπισα, ἤλπικα, --, --.

20. ἔρχομαι (come), ἐλεύσομαι, ἦλθον, ἐλήλυθα, --, --.

21. ἐσθίω (eat), φάγομαι, ἔφαγον, --, --, --.

22. εὑρίσκω (find), εὑρήσω, εὗρον, εὕρηκα, (εὕρημαι), εὑρέθην (smooth breathing can be used, and ην for augment or reduplication).

23. ἔχω (have), ἕξω, ἔσχον, ἔσχηκα, --, -- (imperfect εἶχον).

24. θέλω (will), θελήσω, ἠθέλησα, --, --, -- (imperfect, ἤθελον).

25. θνήσκω (die), θανοῦμαι, ἔθανον, τέθνηκα, --, --.

26. ἵημι (send), ἥσω, ἧκα, εἷκα, εἷμαι, ἕθην.

27. ἵστημι (stand), στήσω, ἔστην or ἔστησα, ἔστηκα, (ἔσταμαι), ἐστάθην (See lexicon for exact meanings of forms.)

28. καλέω (call), καλέσω, ἐκάλεσα, κέκληκα, κέκλημαι, ἐκλήθην.

29. κρίνω (judge), κρινῶ, ἔκρινα, κέκρικα, κέκριμαι, ἐκρίθην.

30. κτείνω (kill), κτενῶ, ἔκτεινα, --, --, ἐκτάνθην.

31. λαμβάνω (take), λήμψομαι, ἔλαβον, εἴληφα, εἴλημμαι, ἐλήμφθην.

32. λέγω (say) or φημί, ἐρῶ, εἶπον, εἴρηκα, εἴρημμαι, ἐρρέθην or ἐρρήθην.

33. λείπω (leave), λείψω, ἔλιπον or ἔλειψα, (λέλοιπα), λέλειμμαι ἐλείφθην.

34. μένω (remain), μενῶ, ἔμεινα, μεμένηκα, --, --.

35. μιμνήσκω (remind), μνήσω, ἔμνησα, (μέμνηκα), μέμνημαι, ἐμνήσθην.

36. ὁράω (see), ὄψομαι, εἶδον, ἑώρακα or ἑόρακα, (ὦμμαι), ὤφθην.

37. πείθω (persuade), πείσω, ἔπεισα, πέποιθα, πέπεισμαι, ἐπείσθην.

38. πίνω (drink), πίομαι, ἔπιον, πέπωκα, --, ἐπόθην.

39. πίπτω (fall), πεσοῦμαι, ἔπεσον, πέπτωκα, --, --.

40. πράσσω (do), πράξω, ἔπραξα, πέπραχα, πέπραγμαι, (ἐπράχθην).

41. σπείρω (sow), (σπερῶ), ἔσπειρα, --, ἔσπαρμαι, ἐσπάρην.

42. στέλλω (send), στελῶ, ἔστειλα, ἔσταλκα, ἔσταλμαι, ἐστάλην.

43. στρέφω (turn), στρέψω, ἔστρεψα, --, ἔστραμμαι, ἐστράφην.

44. τίθημι (place), θήσω, ἔθηκα, τέθεικα, τέθειμαι, ἐτέθην.

45. φέρω (carry), οἴσω, ἤνεγκον, ἐνήνοχα, (ἐνήνεγμαι), ἠνέχθην.

46. χαίρω (rejoice), χαρήσομαι, ἐχάρην, --, --, --.

CHAPTER XIII

THE GRAMMATICAL USAGE OF VERBS

When the student has identified a verb form, he must then know what each factor of that form signifies. We go next, then, to the meaning of person, number, voice, tense and mood.

Section 1

Person

Greek has three persons, just like English. The first person indicates the person speaking, "I" or "we." The second person designates the person spoken to, "you." The third person tells the person spoken about, "he," "she," "it," or "they."

Section 2

Number

Homeric and Classical Greek had three numbers, singular, dual and plural. The dual (for two persons or things) was a luxury that was sinking into disuse in the Classical period and has disappeared in the New Testament period. So we have only the two numbers, singular for one, and plural for more than one.

As in English, the first person plural is used at times when only one person is intended—the editorial we, the we of majesty, or the we of modesty. The context alone can determine whether one or more persons is intended, and at times the context leaves the matter in doubt.

The numbers in the second person are just what they should logically be. The peculiarity of the English second person "you," which may be either singular or plural, makes it difficult to handle this in English, but the Greek is very plain. The

100

Greek has no such distinctions as French or German in the numbers of the second person.

The Greek does have one rather strange idiom in regard to number in the third person. If the subject of the verb is a neuter plural, the verb may be either singular or plural. Of course, even if the verb is singular in Greek it must be translated as a plural in English. ἐξήρχετο δὲ καὶ δαιμόνια ἀπὸ πολλῶν, Lk. 4:41: "And also demons were going out from many."

When a collective noun is the subject, the verb may be either singular or plural, depending upon whether the group as a whole is to be emphasized or the different members in the group. This usage is the same as in English. ἅπαν τὸ πλῆθος αὐτῶν ἤγαγον αὐτὸν ἐπὶ τὸν Πιλᾶτον, Lk. 23:1: "All the crowd of them led him to Pilate."

Compound subjects usually take plural verbs, but the singular may be used if the nearest or most important part of the subject is singular. καὶ ἦν ὁ πατὴρ αὐτοῦ καὶ ἡ μήτηρ ... Lk. 2:33: "And his father and mother were ..."

Section 3

Voice

The Greek language has three voices, active, middle and passive. The active and passive are much the same as in English, regularly denoting that the subject is either acting (active) or is acted upon (passive). "The dog bites," active. "The man is bitten," passive.

The middle voice indicates that the action of the verb starts with the subject and in some way comes back upon the subject. The middle λούομαι means "I bathe myself," a direct reflexive use of the middle, where the subject becomes the direct object. But often it is only an indirect reflexive that is intended, such as συλλέγομαι, meaning "I collect for myself." As there is some chance of ambiguity here, the Greek often uses pronouns as objects or in prepositional phrases, either with the middle or active voice, to make the meaning more definite.

101

Deponent Verbs: Here we are dealing with a phenomenon that we really do not understand. In certain verbs, the Greeks saw some reason for using the middle or passive voice where in English we must use the active voice. ἔρχομαι is middle or passive in Greek, but it means "I come" in English. We give the name "deponent" (out of place) to such verbs. They will be given in the lexicons in the middle or passive form, of course (ἔρχομαι, not ἔρχω).

In those tenses where the middle and passive forms are different (future and aorist), some deponent verbs always use the middle forms, some use the passive, and some use the middle and passive interchangeably. It is not important that the student try to remember which verbs belong in each of these three classes; the matter is, of course, very simple for those verbs for which he knows the principal parts.

Some few verbs are deponent in certain forms and not in others. Again the principal parts will take care of this phenomenon. For example, the principal parts of βαίνω are: βαίνω, βήσομαι, ἔβην, βέβηκα, so we see that it is a middle deponent in the future, while elsewhere it is a regular active verb.

In a very few verbs we find a difference of meaning between the active and the deponent; e.g., ἄρχω means "rule," while ἄρχομαι means "begin." The lexicon will always inform us about such distinctions.

Section 4

Tense

Greek tense has certain things in common with English tenses, but the basic idea of Greek tense is very different from that of English or Latin. The word "tense" comes from the Latin word *tempus*, which means "time," and time is the basic element in tense in English, Latin, and many other languages. But in Greek the basic meaning of tense is not time but kind of action (the German word *aktionsart* is often used even in English grammars for this). Only in the indicative mood does

102

the idea of time regularly come in, and even then it is as a secondary element along with that of kind of action. It is extremely important that the student learn accurately the meaning of the Greek tenses. The translators of the old English versions of the Bible, including the King James, knew their Latin far better than they did their Greek tenses, so they translated the Greek tenses as though they had been Latin. The student who knows his Greek tense can improve on the old translations more at this point than at any other. Even the newer translations show too much dependence upon the King James in the matter of tense, sometimes giving a definitely erroneous idea of the meaning of the Greek, more often failing to bring out shades of meaning seen in the Greek but difficult to bring out in English.

An example of an erroneous translation of the Greek tense at an important point may be seen in I John 3:9, where the King James says that a child of God "cannot sin." That seems to prove sinless perfectionism; and when we do commit acts of sin it seems to prove that we are not children of God. But the tense of the Greek infinitive, the present ἁμαρτάνειν rather then the aorist ἁμαρτῆσαι, makes it clear that John did not mean that at all. He knows that true children of God do from time to time commit acts of sin. But he is trying to drive home the fact that if a man continues in habitual sin he is not a child of God. It is not strange that the King James translators should have made their erroneous translation; it is quite strange, though, that their error should have been perpetuated in the American Standard Version and the Revised Standard Version along with such modern versions as Moffatt and Goodspeed. Weymouth's original version correctly translated it "cannot habitually sin," but the newer revisions of Weymouth sink back into the erroneous "cannot sin." Some of the less well known modern versions handle it correctly.

The student should not get the idea that the King James is full of such important errors and is therefore completely untrustworthy. Most verbs occur in the indicative mood, where tenses in Greek are much like those of Latin. And even in the other moods the King James translation is quite close for all practical purposes. But the careful student of Greek tense can at times correct erroneous translations and can quite often see shades of meaning that the translations do not or even cannot bring out.

Tense in Moods Other than the Indicative

In all the moods other than the indicative (with the minor exception of the future infinitive and participle), Greek tense indicates simply kind of action. There are three kinds of action, and they are brought out by three tenses. A simple diagram will make this plain.

Kind of Action	Name of Tense
Continued (—) or Repeated (...)	Present
Point action (•)	Aorist
State of completion (•—) or (—•)	Perfect

It should be made plain that the kind of action does not depend upon the amount of time involved in the action but upon the way the writer or speaker wishes his reader or hearer to think about the action.

The aorist tense is by far the most common, as it simply states a fact or indicates the action without further defining it (the word "aorist" comes from the Greek, meaning "undefined"). The time involved may be long or short, but the thing is simply looked at as a unit. "He reigned forty years," simply stating the fact of a forty-year reign, would be expressed by the aorist tense.

The present tense spreads the action out as a line or a series of dots. The name "present" is not a good one but is a relic of the time when Greek tense was supposed to indicate time. "He is standing on the street" and "He goes to town three times a day" illustrate this kind of action. It is commonly used in descriptions.

104

The difference between the aorist and present tenses may be made plainer by the illustration of a telescope. Take a telescope and look through it the right way at a house, and the very details of the house become plain, the walls, the windows, the doors, the very bricks that make up the walls; that is like the present tense. Look through the telescope the wrong way, and you see a house; that is like the aorist.

The perfect tense is a combination of a dot and a line. Most often it is a dot followed by a line, indicating a state or a result following an act. "It is written" indicates that the writing is here because somebody wrote it. There are a very few cases of the dot following the line, indicating completion after long or hard effort. The most notable New Testament example of this kind of perfect is found in II Tim. 4:7: τὸν καλὸν ἀγῶνα ἠγώνισμαι, τὸν δρόμον τετέληκα, τὴν πίστιν τετήρηκα, "I have fought the good fight, I have finished the course, I have kept the faith."

For the sake of simplicity, the illustrations for the various kinds of action were given in the indicative mood, where tense shows time as well as kind of action. In the other moods, tense shows kind of action alone, except that there are a future infinitive and a future participle which take the place of the future indicative in certain constructions and thus show future time like the future indicative. It is very important that the student should remember to keep the time element out of the tenses except in the indicative mood. The aorist subjunctive, for example, has nothing whatever to do with past time; aorist indicates point action alone.

The statement is often made that tense in the participle indicates time in relation to the time of the leading verb, but that is really not accurate. Because the aorist participle expresses point action, the point often logically precedes the time of the main verb; but the very common ἀποκριθεὶς εἶπεν gives a very clear example of the dot of the aorist participle coinciding with that of the main verb—"He answered and said."

Tenses in the Indicative Mood

In the indicative mood, the idea of time comes in along with that of kind of action. Historically, the past tenses seem to have developed from the augment, which was an adverb meaning "formerly"; the future tenses seem to have developed from the subjunctive mood, which regularly looks to future time.

As there are three kinds of actions and three times, Greek should logically have developed nine tenses. Actually, however, only seven were developed, so two of the tenses must do double duty: the present indicating either point or linear action in present time, and the future indicating either point or linear action in the future time. Evidently the Greeks did not think it important to distinguish the kind of action in these cases; actually, it is almost impossible logically to have point action in present time.

The following diagram will make plain the tenses used in the indicative mood to bring out the times and kinds of action:

Kind of Action ⌐ Time →	Past	Present	Future
Continued (—) or Repeated (...). .	Imperfect	Present	Future
Point (.)	Aorist	Present	Future
State of Completion (.—) or (—.). .	Pluperfect	Perfect	Future Perfect

The student should get the facts of this diagram well in mind and use them whenever he is interpreting the tense of a verb in the indicative mood. For example, whenever he has an imperfect tense he should immediately think of continued action in past time. After much practice, this will become automatic.

Let us now look at these tenses in somewhat greater detail, noticing also some usages that call for special attention.

106

The Imperfect Tense

The imperfect tense is often used in vivid description. An act in past time is spread out for closer inspection. Customary courses of action in past time are described by the imperfect, or certain acts that were repeated in past time.

The Conative Imperfect: This is used to describe actions that were attempted but not completed. The auxiliary verb "try" should be used to translate this usage. ἐκάλουν αὐτὸ ἐπὶ τῷ ὀνόματι τοῦ πατρός, Lk. 1:59: "They were trying to call him with his father's name." We know, of course, that they finally called the child John instead of Zacharias.

The Inchoative Imperfect: This is used to describe the beginning of an action and should be translated by the use of an auxiliary verb such as "begin." καὶ ἀνοίξας τὸ στόμα αὐτοῦ ἐδίδασκεν αὐτούς, Mt. 5:2: "And opening his mouth he began to teach them."

It should be noted that only the context can determine whether the simple translation or one of the less common ones should be used. That will be true in all the other tenses as well as in the imperfect.

The Aorist Tense

The aorist simply states a fact in past time without further defining it. The action may have taken only a moment of time or may have been of long duration, but the aorist tense merely looks at it as a unit. The aorist tense is by far the most common one to use in narrative relating to past time.

The Epistolary Aorist: Here we have an idiom different from anything we have in English. In a letter, the writer may out of courtesy put himself in the time of the receiver of the letter, so he can speak of the time of the writing as past and use the aorist to describe it. Ἴδετε πηλίκοις ὑμῖν γράμμασιν ἔγραψα τῇ ἐμῇ χειρί, Gal. 6:11: "See with what large letters I am writing with my own hand." In English, of course, we must translate an epistolary aorist with a present. Only the context enables

107

us to spot this use of the aorist. At times in letters the context is not definite enough to enable us to know whether the aorist refers to the present letter or to a previous one, so an ambiguity results.

The Gnomic Aorist: The Greek language can use the aorist tense as well as the present in proverbial statements or other truths of universal time. In English we must use the present tense to translate the gnomic aorist. Grammarians cannot explain why the Greeks used this aorist, but it is well established that they did. οὗτός ἐστιν ὁ υἱός μου ὁ ἀγαπητός, ἐν ᾧ εὐδόκησα, Mt. 3:17: "This is my beloved Son in whom I am well pleased."

The Ingressive (or Inceptive) Aorist: This is often used with verbs whose root meaning is continued action to indicate the point at which the action began. ἀλληλουϊά, ὅτι ἐβασίλευσεν κύριος ὁ θεὸς ἡμῶν, Rev. 19:6: "Hallelujah, because the Lord our God has become king." It is possible that this aorist may be the gnomic, referring to the eternal reign of God, but it is probable that in this context it refers to the time when God begins the full reign over the new heaven and the new earth.

The Prophetic Aorist: At times a prophet will use the aorist to describe something that has not happened but which he is so sure will happen that he speaks of it as though it had. ἔπεσεν ἔπεσεν Βαβυλὼν ἡ μεγάλη, Rev. 18:2: "Babylon the great has fallen, has fallen," John could say concerning Rome when Rome was at the height of its power. In English we may use a past tense for translation if we understand the idiom, or we may use a simple future to prevent misunderstanding.

At times several of these usages may overlap; for example, the aorist in Rev. 19:6 is a prophetic as well as an ingressive aorist.

The Pluperfect Tense

The Greek pluperfect is not the same as the English pluperfect. The English pluperfect often indicates a dot preceding another dot: "When he had stood up he left the room." For that the Greek would use simply two aorists.

108

The Greek pluperfect is used only rarely, to indicate that the line coming out of the dot went to some designated time in the past. σκοτία ἤδη ἐγεγόνει καὶ οὔπω ἐληλύθει πρὸς αὐτοὺς ὁ Ἰησοῦς, John 6:17: "Darkness had already come, and Jesus had not yet come to them."

There are some few Greek verbs whose perfect tenses are translated like presents, such as οἶδα, "I know." Their pluperfects will be translated, then, like a past tense of some kind, either aorist, imperfect or pluperfect. κἀγὼ οὐκ ᾔδειν αὐτόν, John 1:31: "And I did not know him."

The Present Tense

The present tense in Greek is used much like the present in English, to indicate an action or a state going on at the present time. It is regularly used for proverbial or universal statements, though the gnomic aorist may also be used. The present indicative may indicate either linear or point action in present time, though logically point action in present time is not often used.

The Historical Present: This is used in Greek as in English. For the sake of vividness, the narrator describes the past as though it were the present. It is usually wise to translate such presents with an English present. Some writers, like Mark, are rather careless about mixing historical presents and simple aorists, so most translators try to improve on their style by changing the aorists into historical presents or vice versa. The student may read the paragraph Mk. 4:35–41 as a good example of a mixture of the historical presents and the regular past tenses, aorists and imperfects.

The Futuristic Present: This is found at times in Greek as in English. "He is going to town tomorrow," we often say rather than "He will go." A temporal adverb or some other feature of the context will make this plain. τί ποιοῦμεν; ὅτι οὗτος ὁ ἄνθρωπος πολλὰ ποιεῖ σημεῖα, John 11:47: "What shall we do? Because this man is performing many signs." The verb ἔρχομαι often uses the present with a future meaning as the corresponding verb does in English.

The Conative Present.   This indicates an attempt made rather than an accomplished fact. ἢ τοῦ πλούτου τῆς χρηστότητος αὐτοῦ... καταφρονεῖς, ἀγνοῶν ὅτι τὸ χρηστὸν τοῦ θεοῦ εἰς μετάνοιάν σε ἄγει; Rom. 2:4: "Or do you despise the wealth of His kindness, not knowing that the goodness of God is trying to lead you to repentance?"   The auxiliary verb "try" should normally be used to translate the conative present.

The Perfect Tense

The perfect tense is used to call attention to some kind of result in present time coming from some preceding act, or in a few cases a result attained after long or diligent effort, as in Paul's "I have fought a good fight..." (II Tim. 4:7). καθὼς γέγραπται ἐν τῷ 'Ησαΐᾳ τῷ προφήτῃ, Mk, 1:2: "As it is written in Isaiah the prophet."   Isaiah wrote; in Mark's day he could say, "Here it is, written."   In the active voice we translate the Greek perfect with the help of the English auxiliary verb "have."   In the passive, however, the verb "be" often brings out the meaning even better; "It is written" is better than "It has been written," as it clearly brings out the present result.   That is not to be confused with the present passive, "It is being written," meaning that the writing is going on at the present time.

The Blending of the Perfect and the Aorist Tenses: Latin did not have two tenses corresponding to the Greek aorist and perfect.   In Greek of the *koine* period the perfect seems to be dying.   There are times, especially in the later books of the New Testament, when the perfect seems to be used just like an aorist, calling attention to the past act but not the present result. καὶ ἦλθεν καὶ εἴληφεν ἐκ τῆς δεξιᾶς τοῦ καθημένου ἐπὶ τοῦ θρόνου, Rev. 5:7: "And he came and took it from the right hand of the one sitting upon the throne."   Some good grammarians would argue this point, believing that they can always see something of the present result in every perfect in the New Testament; it is certainly true that the vast majority of perfects show some present result.

The Future Tense

The future tense is used to indicate future time, either in continued or point action. As in the present, the Greeks did not develop different tenses for the two different kinds of action.

There is nothing in Greek quite like the English distinction between shall and will in the different persons. When emphasis, will, or determination is desired, the Greek must indicate that by the use of adverbs or auxiliary verbs.

The Imperative Use of the Future Indicative: As in English, the future indicative is often used in commands. In the Greek Old Testament the future indicative is used in the Ten Commandments. ἠκούσατε ὅτι ἐρρέθη· ἀγαπήσεις τὸν πλησίον σου καὶ μισήσεις τὸν ἐχθρόν σου, Mt. 5:43: "You have heard that it was said, 'Love your neighbor and hate your enemy.'"

The Deliberative Use of the Future: There is, of course, the deliberative subjunctive, but at times the future indicative is used to consult the judgment of another person. κύριε, ποσάκις ἁμαρτήσει εἰς ἐμὲ ὁ ἀδελφός μου καὶ ἀφήσω αὐτῷ; Mt. 18:21: "Lord, how often shall my brother sin against me and I will forgive him?"

The Future Perfect Tense

The future perfect is used very seldom in the New Testament. It puts the completion of the action into future time. ἐγὼ ἔσομαι πεποιθὼς ἐπ' αὐτῷ, Heb. 2:13: "I shall have trusted on him." ὃ ἐὰν δήσῃς ἐπὶ τῆς γῆς ἔσται δεδεμένον ἐν τοῖς οὐρανοῖς, Mt. 16:19: "Whatever you bind on earth shall have been bound in heaven."

The future perfect εἰδήσουσιν in Heb. 8:11 is to be translated like a simple future, as the perfect οἶδα means the present "I know."

Section 5

Mood

The Greek verb has six moods, or modes: the indicative, the subjunctive, the optative, the imperative, the infinitive, and the

111

participle. Not all grammarians consider the infinitive and the participle verbal moods, as the infinitive is a verbal noun and the participle a verbal adjective.

Those who are familiar with Classical Greek will find quite a few differences in the use of the moods when they come to the *koine* period. In the *koine*, for example, the optative mood is almost gone; the subjunctive mood is taking over its usages. Also the future indicative is often used instead of a subjunctive. And other minor differences appear from time to time.

The Indicative Mood

The indicative is the easiest, and yet in a sense the most difficult, of the moods to handle. In general, we can say that the indicative is the mood to use when there is no reason for using any other mood. It is by far the most common, normal mood, used very much like the indicative mood in English.

The indicative is the normal mood for simple declarative statements. Numerous examples are found on every page of the New Testament.

The indicative is the normal mood in simple questions. Questions with a positive or negative expectation also use the indicative mood, accompanied by οὐ for the positive expectation and μή for the negative. See the fuller treatment of the adverbs οὐ and μή, page 52. Deliberative questions use the subjunctive mood regularly, but at times the future indicative.

The future indicative is often used to give commands, as we saw under the future tense.

The future indicative is often used in the *koine* period in many constructions in place of a subjunctive mood. It will be most convenient to deal with these usages under the subjunctive mood and under the appropriate clauses. As the future indicative is so similar in form to the aorist subjunctive (and, historically, probably developed from it), it is not surprising that it should come to be used in place of it, particularly in dependent clauses after conjunctions. As a further extension,

112

there are a very few examples of the present indicative doing the regular work of a subjunctive: ἵνα γινώσκομεν τὸν ἀληθινόν, I John 5:20: "In order that we may know the one who is true."

The indicative mood is used in both the protasis and the apodosis of simple conditions, and in either the protasis or apodosis of other types of conditional sentences. See the fuller treatment of conditional sentences on pages 122ff.

The indicative is used in various subordinate clauses, much as it is in English. The indicative mood should be used unless there is some special reason for using some other. The various types of clauses are treated more fully on pages 121f.

The Subjunctive Mood

It is impossible to give any one translation to the subjunctive mood. It has some usages that are somewhat similar to the subjunctive in English, but Greek used the subjunctive far more than we do in modern English. The only way to handle the mood in Greek is to know its various usages and the translation that is appropriate to each one.

1. The Hortatory Subjunctive: The first person plural of the subjunctive is used to express exhortations. ἐγείρεσθε, ἄγωμεν ἐντεῦθεν, John 14:31: "Arise, let us go hence." As the English does not have this usage, we must translate it with the aid of an auxiliary verb, "let," and put the Greek subject, if it is expressed, in the English accusative. And the student should be careful to distinguish between this "Let us go," which is an exhortation, and the "Let us go," which is a command or an entreaty meaning "Permit us to go," which would be expressed very differently in Greek.

2. Deliberative Questions: Simple questions use the indicative mood, but the subjunctive is used to indicate uncertainty or deliberation. σὺ εἶ ὁ ἐρχόμενος, ἢ ἄλλον προσδοκῶμεν; Lk. 7:19: "Are you the coming one, or shall we look for another one?" This usage may likewise use the first person plural when it is appropriate. When it does, there is a possibility of some confusion with the hortatory subjunctive, when we remember

113

that the punctuation marks were not in the earliest manuscripts and that each interpreter is free to supply whatever he thinks best. ἐπιμένωμεν τῇ ἁμαρτίᾳ in Rom. 6:1 may well be handled in either way: "Let us remain in sin" or "Shall we remain in sin?" When anything other than the first person plural is used, though, there can be no such confusion.

3. The Subjunctive of Prohibition: A positive command is expressed by the imperative mood. A negative command, though, is expressed by μή and the present imperative (for continued action, or the stopping of an action that had been continued) or by μή and the aorist subjunctive (for punctiliar action). μὴ νομίσητε ὅτι ἦλθον καταλῦσαι τὸν νόμον ἢ τοὺς προφήτας, Mt. 5:17: "Do not think that I came to destroy the law or the prophets." We do not know why the Greeks did not use μή and the aorist imperative, but they saw fit to use uniformly μή and the aorist subjunctive instead. At times they also used οὐ with the future indicative in negative commands.

4. Emphatic Future Negations: A very emphatic negation in future time is expressed by οὐ μή and the subjunctive mood. ἀμὴν γὰρ λέγω ὑμῖν, οὐ μὴ τελέσητε τὰς πόλεις τοῦ ᾽Ισραὴλ ἕως ἔλθῃ ὁ υἱὸς τοῦ ἀνθρώπου, Mt. 10:23: "Verily I say to you, 'You will not finish the cities of Israel until the son of man comes.'"

5. Subjunctive in Conditional Sentences: εἰ and the modal sign ἄν (usually contracted to ἐάν or even ἄν) are used with the subjunctive mood in the protases (the clauses containing the "if") of future more vivid and present general conditions. See pages 122ff. for a fuller treatment of the whole subject of conditional sentences.

6. Indefinite Relative Clauses: An indefinite relative clause may be expressed by the use of some relative word, the modal sign ἄν (sometimes, illogically, ἐάν), and the subjunctive mood of the verb. This usage is called the conditional relative clause by some. εἰς ἣν δ᾽ἂν πόλιν ἢ κώμην ε᾽ισέλθητε, Mt. 10:11: "And into whatever city or village you enter . . ." This usage is translated by adding an "ever" or "soever" to whatever

the relative word may be in English. At times the modal sign
and the relative word may be contracted, such as ὅτε and ἄν
becoming ὅταν. The relative word may be a pronoun, adjective,
adverb, or conjunction. Greek has some indefinite relative
words, such as ὅστις, which can be used either with the
indicative mood or with ἄν and the subjunctive for even more
indefiniteness.

7. Future Temporal Clauses: Temporal clauses referring to
future time are often expressed by the use of an appropriate
conjunction, with or without the modal sign ἄν (or ἐάν), and
the subjunctive mood of the verb. κἀκεῖ μείνατε ἕως ἂν ἐξέλθητε,
Mt. 10:11: "And remain there until you leave." The English
can use the subjunctive in such a construction ("Till He come."),
but it more often uses the indicative ("Till He comes."). The
Greek at times uses the future indicative in such clauses.

8. Purpose (and Extensions): Purpose is often expressed
by ἵνα (less commonly, ὅπως or ὡς) and the subjunctive mood
of the verb. μὴ κρίνετε, ἵνα μὴ κριθῆτε, Mt. 7:1: "Do not be
always judging, in order that you may not be judged." There
are several other ways of expressing purpose, but this is one of
the most common. At times the future indicative is used instead
of the subjunctive; a very few times even the present indicative.

When the student sees a ἵνα with a subjunctive, he should
first try to translate it "in order that," thereby making it a
purpose clause. But often such a translation will not fit the
context at all, so "that" must be used instead. συμφέρει γάρ
σοι ἵνα ἀπόληται ἓν τῶν μελῶν σου, Mt. 5:29: "For it is profit-
able for you that one of your members should perish." In the
koine period this extension of the purpose idea is very common;
it can do almost anything that a "that" clause can do in
English.

9. Result: There are various ways of expressing result in
Greek, but ἵνα with the subjunctive seems to be used very
rarely. ῥαββί, τίς ἥμαρτεν, οὗτος ἢ οἱ γονεῖς αὐτοῦ, ἵνα τυφλὸς
γεννηθῇ; John 9:2: "Rabbi, who sinned, this man or his parents,
so that he was born blind?" This usage is debated; some

115

grammarians would consider all examples of it really purpose clauses.

10.   Object Clauses After Verbs of Fearing: μή with the subjunctive is used after verbs of fearing. φοβηθῶμεν οὖν μήποτε ... δοκῇ τις ἐξ ὑμῶν ὑστερηκέναι, Heb. 4:1: "Let us fear, therefore, lest perchance any one of you may seem to have come short."

The Optative Mood

In the *koine* period the optative mood is dying out, but it is not quite gone.

1.   The Optative of Wish: Wishes, both positive and negative (with μή) may be expressed by the optative mood. This is the most common usage of the optative, and by far the most common example is Paul's μὴ γένοιτο (Rom. 3:4 and throughout his epistles): "May it not be," or according to the King James' paraphrase, "God forbid."

2.   The Potential Optative: The optative, usually with the modal sign ἄν, may be translated by a "should" or "would," or a "may" or "might." This rather literary usage is found in the New Testament only in Luke and Acts. ἐπηρώτων δὲ αὐτὸν οἱ μαθηταὶ αὐτοῦ τίς αὕτη εἴη ἡ παραβολή, Lk. 8:9: "And his disciples kept asking him what this parable might be."

3.   The Optative in Future Less Vivid Conditional Sentences: The protasis has εἰ and the optative mood, while the apodosis has the optative and the modal sign ἄν. See the fuller treatment of conditional sentences on pages 122ff.

The Imperative Mood

The imperative mood in Greek, as in English, is used for the purpose of giving commands, making entreaties, or granting permission.   Jesus can command, διαλλάγηθι τῷ ἀδελφῷ σου, Mt. 5:24: "Be reconciled to your brother." And we can entreat God, τὸν ἄρτον ἡμῶν τὸν ἐπιούσιον δὸς ἡμῖν σήμερον, Mt. 6:11: "Give us this day our daily bread."

The student should remember that negative commands

116

(prohibitions) are expressed with μή and the present imperative, or with μή and the aorist subjunctive. The present imperative is used when continued action is meant. It may be either a command not to make a practice of doing something, as in Mt. 7:1, μὴ κρίνετε, "Do not be always judging," or a command to stop something that has been going on, as probably, μὴ μεριμνᾶτε τῇ ψυχῇ ὑμῶν τί φάγητε, Mt. 6:25: "Stop worrying about your life, what you will eat."

Greek has the third person of the imperative, but it is necessary to translate it periphrastically in English. ἁγιασθήτω τὸ ὄνομά σου· ἐλθάτω ἡ βασιλεία σου, Mt. 6:9–10: "Let thy name be hallowed; let thy kingdom come." Notice that the subject of the imperative is in the nominative case in Greek; do not be confused by the English accusative, such as "Let him do it." And remember that the English "Let him do it," may be either the imperative of the verb "do," or "Permit him to do it," thoughts that would be expressed very differently in the Greek.

The Infinitive Mood

The infinitive is a mood of the verb, and it is also a noun. It is basically the same as the infinitive in English, but there are some usages that are somewhat different and call for special notice.

As a verb form, the infinitive has voice (active, middle and passive) and tense (aorist, present, perfect and future--all except the last showing kind of action only). It can have a subject (in the accusative case) and have a direct or indirect object, and can be modified by adverbs or prepositional phrases.

As a noun, the infinitive can be in any case (though the vocative is logically never used). It is indeclinable and is always considered neuter in gender. It may be modified by adjectives, particularly the definite article. The infinitive may be used as a subject or object of the verb, or as the object of certain prepositions. Many of these Greek usages would be

117

translated in English by the gerund ending in -ing, such as "Running is good exercise."

The infinitive is often used to express indirect discourse. Its subject will, of course, be in the accusative case. If the infinitive is the verb "to be" or any other copula, it may be followed by the predicate accusative. τίνα λέγουσιν οἱ ἄνθρωποι εἶναι τὸν υἱὸν τοῦ ἀνθρώπου; Mt. 16:13: "Who do men say that the son of man is?" We may use the infinitive for the English translation, but usually it is much more idiomatic to use a clause introduced by "that."

The infinitive may be used to complete the idea begun in various words. εἴ τις θέλει ὀπίσω μου ἐλθεῖν, Mt. 16:24: "If anyone wishes to come after me ..."

Purpose may be expressed in various ways by using the infinitive:

(a) The simple infinitive: ὥσπερ ὁ υἱὸς τοῦ ἀνθρώπου οὐκ ἦλθεν διακονηθῆναι, ἀλλὰ διακονῆσαι καὶ δοῦναι τὴν ψυχὴν αὐτοῦ, Mt. 20:28: "Just as the son of man did not come to be served but to serve and to give his life ..."

(b) The infinitive as the object of the prepositions εἰς or πρός: εἰς τὸ εἶναι αὐτὸν δίκαιον, Rom. 3:26: "In order that he may be righteous."

(c) The genitive of the articular infinitive: ἰδοὺ ἐξῆλθεν ὁ σπείρων τοῦ σπείρειν, Mt. 13:3: "Behold, the sower went forth to sow."

The temporal idea may be expressed by the infinitive after various prepositions. μετὰ τὸ παθεῖν αὐτόν, Acts 1:3: "After he had suffered ..." ἐν τῷ ἱερατεύειν αὐτόν, Lk. 1:8: "While he was acting as priest ..." διὰ παντὸς τοῦ ζῆν, Heb. 2:15: "Throughout all their lives ..."

Result is often expressed by ὥστε with the infinitive. καὶ ἐθεράπευσεν αὐτοὺς ὥστε τὸν ὄχλον θαυμάσαι, Mt. 15:31: "And he healed them, so that the crowd was amazed."

The Participle

As the infinitive is a verbal noun, the participle is a verbal adjective. It is basically the same as the participle in English.

118

As a verb, the participle has voice and tense, and can have objects and modifying adverbs and prepositional phrases.

As an adjective, it can modify nouns and can act as a noun. Unlike the Greek infinitive, the Greek participle is fully declined, showing case, number and gender.

The Greek language uses the participle much more frequently than we do in English. It also uses it in constructions that are so complex that we find it better or even necessary to handle them in English by various clauses.

The participle with the article is usually best translated by an English relative clause. ὁ μὴ τιμῶν τὸν υἱὸν οὐ τιμᾷ τὸν πατέρα τὸν πέμψαντα αὐτόν, John 5:23: "The one who does not honor the son does not honor the father who sent him." Here the first participle is used as the subject of the main verb, and the second one modifies the direct object.

The participle without the article may be translated by an English participle or a clause, usually temporal. ἐπάρας οὖν τοὺς ὀφθαλμοὺς ὁ Ἰησοῦς καὶ θεασάμενος, John 6:5: "So Jesus, having lifted up his eyes and seen . . ." or "So when Jesus had lifted up his eyes and seen . . ." Clauses other then temporal ones may at times be indicated by the context.

The student should remember the use of the participle as the verbal element in the genitive and accusative absolute constructions. See pages 33 and 38.

CHAPTER XIV

SENTENCES AND CLAUSES

Most of what might be discussed under this heading has already been handled under the usages of the various parts of speech, particularly the verb. Here will be given largely outlines and references to the places where the various constructions are described.

No attempt is made to give a complete list of the different types of sentences and clauses, as many are just the same as in English and can easily be handled without special treatment.

Section 1

Questions

1. Simple questions. Indicative mood of the verb. May be introduced by various interrogative words--pronouns, adjectives, adverbs.

2. Deliberative questions. Subjunctive mood of the verb. See page 113ff. Rarely the future indicative is used. See page 111.

3. Questions expecting positive answer (introduced by *οὐ*) or negative answer (introduced by *μή*). See page 52f.

4. Indirect questions. May be of any type as direct questions. Keep the same tense and mood as would have been used in the corresponding direct question. It may be necessary to change the person. *μὴ μεριμνᾶτε τῇ ψυχῇ ὑμῶν τί φάγητε ἢ τί πίητε,* Mt. 6:25: "Stop worrying about your life, what you shall eat or what you shall drink." The corresponding direct question would have been, *τί φάγωμεν ἢ τί πίωμεν;* "What shall we eat or what shall we drink?"

Section 2

Purpose Clauses

1. With ἵνα *(ὅπως* or *ὡς)* and the subjunctive. See p. 115.
2. With ἵνα *(ὅπως* or *ὡς)* and the future indicative. See p. 115. (Rarely even a present indicative. See p. 113).
3. With εἰς or πρός and the accusative of the articular infinitive. See p. 118.
4. With the genitive of the articular infinitive. See p. 118.
5. With the simple infinitive. See p. 118.

Section 3

Result Clauses

1. With ὥστε (rarely ὅτι) and the indicative mood. οὕτως γὰρ ἠγάπησεν ὁ θεὸς τὸν κόσμον, ὥστε τὸν υἱὸν τὸν μονογενῆ ἔδωκεν, John 3:16: "God so loved the world that He gave his only son . . ."
2. With ὥστε and the infinitive, with the subject of the infinitive being, of course, in the accusative case. κἂν ἔχω πᾶσαν τὴν πίστιν ὥστε ὄρη μεθιστάνειν, I Cor. 13:2: "And if I have all faith so as to remove mountains."
3. Rarely with ἵνα and the subjunctive. See p. 115.

Section 4

Temporal Clauses

1. Referring to past or present time:
   a. With a temporal conjunction and the indicative mood of the verb. ὅτε ἐτέλεσεν ὁ Ἰησοῦς τοὺς λόγους τούτους, μετῆρεν, Mt. 19:1: "When Jesus had finished these words, he departed."
   b. With a preposition and the articular infinitive. See p. 118.
2. Referring to future time:
   a. With ἕως (with or without ἄν) and the subjunctive mood of the verb. See p. 115.

b. With ἕως (with or without ἄν) and the future indicative. See p. 115.

3. Referring to indefinite time: ὅτε plus ἄν (ὅταν) and the subjunctive mood (rarely the indicative mood). See p. 114f.

Section 5

Conditional Sentences

	Protasis (if)	Apodosis
1. Simple	εἰ with indicative	indicative
2. Future more Vivid	ἐάν with subjunctive	future indicative or equivalent
3. Present General	ἐάν with subjunctive	present indicative or equivalent
4. Future less Vivid	εἰ with optative	optative with ἄν
5. Present Contrary to Fact	εἰ with imperfect indicative	imperfect indicative with ἄν
6. Past Contrary to Fact	εἰ with aorist or pluperfect indic.	aorist or pluperfect indicative with ἄν

7. Incomplete
8. Mixed

It will be most helpful to the student if he gets this outline firmly fixed in mind. It is necessary to identify the type of conditional sentence used before it can be accurately translated.

We shall now consider each type of conditional sentence in some detail.

1. The simple condition. This is a pure conditional construction, without any implications of possibility, probability or actuality. It may refer to any time or combination of times. The protasis uses the simple εἰ and the indicative mood in any appropriate tense. The apodosis uses the indicative mood or any equivalent, such as the imperative or the hortatory subjunctive. εἰ δὲ ἡ ἀδικία ἡμῶν θεοῦ δικαιοσύνην συνίστησιν, τί ἐροῦμεν; Rom. 3:5: "But if our unrighteousness establishes the righteousness of God, what shall we say?"

2. The future more vivid condition. This will be in contrast with the future less vivid. In the more vivid construction there is an implication that the speaker or writer believes that there is a likelihood of the condition being fulfilled. It is difficult or impossible to bring out this implication in an English translation. But the interpreter may well keep in mind the implied probability. Of course, the implied probability is not always fulfilled, but the writer uses this particular type to show that he believes that it will probably occur. At times, however, the writer seems to use this type just as though it were a simple future condition, with no implication of probability at all implied. Mt. 6:22–23 gives an example of two such conditions giving both alternatives: ἐὰν οὖν ᾖ ὁ ὀφθαλμός σου ἁπλοῦς, ὅλον τὸ σῶμά σου φωτεινὸν ἔσται. ἐὰν δὲ ὁ ὀφθαλμός σου πονηρὸς ᾖ, ὅλον τὸ σῶμά σου σκοτεινὸν ἔσται: "If, then, your eye is single, your whole body will be light; but if your eye is evil, your whole body will be dark." Jesus is not implying the probability of the eye being either good or bad. Probability, though, seems implied in Mt. 9:21, when the woman says: ἐὰν μόνον ἅψωμαι τοῦ ἱματίου αὐτοῦ σωθήσομαι: "If only I touch his garment, I shall be healed."

3. The present general condition. This type has the same ἐάν and the subjunctive in the protasis as did the former type. But here we have in the apodosis a present indicative or its equivalent. Thus a general truth is expressed in a conditional form. καὶ ἐὰν ἀσπάσησθε τοὺς ἀδελφοὺς ὑμῶν μόνον, τί περισσὸν ποιεῖτε; Mt. 5:47: "And if you greet only your brothers, what are you doing superior?"

At times it may be impossible to distinguish between the future more vivid and the present general, when the apodosis uses something that may be the equivalent of either the future indicative or the present indicative, such as an imperative or a hortatory subjunctive, which may give the idea of both futurity and general truth. The translations of the two ideas can be made the same, but the interpreter may remain in doubt as to just what shade of meaning the original author intended. ἐὰν οὖν προσφέρῃς τὸ δῶρόν σου ἐπὶ τὸ θυσιαστήριον κἀκεῖ μνησθῇς ὅτι ὁ ἀδελφός σου ἔχει τι κατὰ σοῦ, ἄφες ἐκεῖ τὸ δῶρόν σου ἔμπροσθεν τοῦ θυσιαστηρίου..., Mt. 5:23–24: "So if you are bringing your gift to the altar and there remember that your brother has something against you, leave your gift there before the altar..." This makes excellent sense as a future more vivid in the case of an individual and also as a general truth.

4. Future less vivid condition. Here the author wants to imply improbability. That can be easily brought out by the English "should" and "would." εἰ with the optative is found in the protasis, and the apodosis has the optative with the modal sign ἄν. As the optative is almost a dead mood in the New Testament period, we do not find a single full example of this type in the New Testament, but only a few fragments such as in I Peter 3:14: ἀλλ᾿ εἰ καὶ πάσχοιτε διὰ δικαιοσύνην, μακάριοι: "But even if you should suffer for the sake of righteousness, happy (would you be)."

5. Present contrary to fact condition. Here the author clearly states that he believes that the condition is not true. "...if he were... (but we know that he is not)." The protasis uses εἰ with the imperfect indicative, while the apodosis uses the imperfect indicative with the modal sign ἄν. οὗτος εἰ ἦν ὁ προφήτης, ἐγίνωσκεν ἂν τίς καὶ ποταπὴ ἡ γυνὴ ἥτις ἅπτεται αὐτοῦ, Lk. 7:39: "If this man were a prophet, he would know who and what kind of woman it is who touches him." And the man is quite sure in his own mind that Jesus is not the prophet. It may seem strange that the Greek uses an imperfect for a present contrary to fact condition, but the English does much the same: "If he were (not, of course, 'was')... it would be..." (but he is not). We may notice that the author may be wrong in his estimate of the true facts.

6. Past contrary to fact condition. This is similar, except that it uses εἰ with either the aorist or pluperfect in the protasis and the aorist or pluperfect with ἄν in the apodosis, to indicate the belief that the thing expressed in the condition was not

true at some past time. "If it had been . . . it would have been . . ." (but, of course, it was not). εἰ ἐγνώκειτέ με, καὶ τὸν πατέρα μου ἂν ᾔδειτε, John 14:7: "If you had known me, you would have also known my Father."

7. Incomplete conditions. There are times when the apodosis may not be expressed. At times this is clearly done on purpose as a very effective figure of speech, aposiopesis. "If you do this . . ." may be much more powerful than the full sentence would have been. At times, though, the lack of completion may be due to carelessness; the author gets involved in a long, complicated construction and then just does not finish it. In Rom. 2:17 Paul starts a conditional sentence, εἰ δὲ σὺ Ἰουδαῖος ἐπονομάζῃ, "But if you call yourself a Jew," but the sentence runs on and on, and no formal apodosis is ever introduced.

8. Mixed conditions. At times the author begins to use one type of conditional sentence and then for some reason, usually in a long, involved sentence, concludes by using another type. Again this may be a very effective rhetorical device or just a careless slip. εἰ ἔχετε πίστιν ὡς κόκκον σινάπεως, ἐλέγετε ἂν τῇ συκαμίνῳ ταύτῃ, Lk. 17:6: "If you have faith as a mustard seed, you would say to this sycamore tree." The protasis is a simple, while the apodosis is a present contrary to fact condition.

In a few cases minor irregularities may be seen, such as the omission of the modal sign ἄν when it is regularly used, or its insertion where it is not needed, or the use of the future indicative instead of a subjunctive. These things, though, will not affect the translation or interpretation. The vast majority of conditional sentences will fall very exactly into the six regular classes; if the student knows them, he can very easily handle the few irregularities that may arise.

Section 6

Direct and Indirect Discourse

1. Direct Discourse:

Here the exact words of the original speaker or writer are given. πάλιν οὖν αὐτοῖς ἐλάλησεν ὁ ᾽Ιησοῦς λέγων· ἐγώ εἰμι τὸ φῶς τοῦ κόσμου, John 8:12: "So Jesus again spoke to them, saying, 'I am the light of the world.'"

Quotation marks are not used in editions of the Greek New Testament, so we do not have their help in identifying direct discourse. We should use them in the English translation.

ὅτι recitative. ὅτι, which is regularly used in indirect discourse, is at times used also to introduce direct discourse. It should not be translated, as English does not use a "that" to introduce direct discourse. λέγουσιν αὐτῷ ὅτι πάντες ζητοῦσίν σε, Mk. 1:37: "They say to him: 'All men are looking for you.'"

2. Indirect Discourse:

    a. After ὅτι. This construction is almost the same as English usage with one important difference. The Greek regularly keeps the same tense in the indirect discourse that was used in the direct discourse, whereas English makes an adaptation of tense after a past tense of the verb of saying; at times the Greek makes the same adaptation as we do in English. ἐφοβήθη ἐπιγνοὺς ὅτι ῾Ρωμαῖός ἐστιν καὶ ὅτι αὐτὸν ἦν δεδεκώς, Acts 22:29: "He was afraid when he recognized that he was a Roman and that he had bound him." This is an example of both usages; the ἐστιν retains the tense of the direct discourse, while the ἦν δεδεκώς, an analytical pluperfect, reflects a perfect in the direct discourse.

    b. With the infinitive. See p. 118. τίνα λέγουσιν οἱ ἄνθρωποι εἶναι τὸν υἱὸν τοῦ ἀνθρώπου Mt. 16:13: "Who do men say that the son of man is?"

    c. With the participle. See p. 118f. ἀκούομεν γάρ τινας

περιπατοῦντας ἐν ὑμῖν ἀτάκτως, II Thes. 3:11: "For we hear that certain ones among you are living disorderly."

d. Rarely with ἵνα or ὅπως and the subjunctive (See the extension of the purpose use of the subjunctive, p. 115). παρήγγειλεν αὐτοῖς ἵνα μηδὲν αἴρωσιν, Mk. 6:8: "He commanded them that they should take nothing."

Section 7

Relative Clauses

1. Simple relative clauses. Some relative word followed by the indicative mood. See relative pronouns, p. 49f. ἐφανέρωσά σου τὸ ὄνομα τοῖς ἀνθρώποις οὓς ἔδωκας μοί, John 17:6: "I have manifested thy name to the men whom thou gavest me."

2. Indefinite relative clauses. Some relative word, the modal sign ἄν, and the subjunctive mood. See p. 114f. εἰς ἣν δ' ἄν πόλιν ἢ κώμην εἰσέλθητε, Mt. 10:11: "Into whatever city or village you enter . . ."

Section 8

Causal Clauses

1. A causal conjunction (ὅτι, γάρ, διότι, ἐπεί, etc.) and the indicative mood. ὅτι ἐγὼ ζῶ καὶ ὑμεῖς ζήσετε, Jn. 14:19: "Because I live, you too will live."

2. διά and the accusative of the articular infinitive. αὐτὸς δὲ Ἰησοῦς οὐκ ἐπίστευεν αὐτὸν αὐτοῖς διὰ τὸ αὐτὸν γινώσκειν πάντας, Jn. 2:24: "But Jesus himself would not entrust himself to them because he knew all men."

3. The participle. Either a simple circumstantial participle (p. 118f.) or a genitive absolute construction (p. 33). μὴ θέλων αὐτὴν δειγματίσαι, ἐβουλήθη λάθρα ἀπολῦσαι αὐτήν, Mt. 1:19: "Since he did not wish to make her a public example, he decided to put her away secretly."

127

CHAPTER XV

THE GREEK OF THE NEW TESTAMENT

Many students come to the study of New Testament Greek after they have studied Homeric or Classical Greek. Certain differences can easily be seen. For a time there was considerable debate as to the nature of the Greek of the New Testament.

There were some who believed that New Testament Greek was a special language invented by God's Spirit for the definite purpose of recording His revelation to mankind. But God wanted His revelation to be understood by men, so it is most unreasonable to believe that He would have recorded it in a new language that men did not know.

Others believed that the Greek of the New Testament was a crude mixture of Greek and Aramaic, written by Jews who knew very little Greek. There is, of course, a measure of truth in this theory, but a very small measure.

At the end of the last century and the beginning of the present one, great quantities of papyrus documents of all kinds were discovered. They had been buried for centuries under the sand in dry Egypt or under the volcanic dust of Mt. Vesuvius in Italy. Many of these documents contained exact dates, and many of them were in Greek. The German scholar, Adolf Deissmann, came to see that the Greek of the papyri contemporaneous with the New Testament was really the same as the Greek of the New Testament. He published a number of books demonstrating this conclusively, the best known of which was his "Light from the Ancient East," (English translation in 1910 from the German "Licht vom Osten" of 1908). Deissmann's views were universally accepted almost immediately.

Languages are never static things. We do not speak the English of the time of Chaucer or even of Shakespeare. The

New Testament writers did not write Homeric Greek or Classical Greek but the Greek that was in normal use at their own time.

Students of historical Greek grammar divide the Greek language into several major divisions:

1. Homeric Greek: About 1000 B.C. the two great Homeric epics were written, the Iliad and the Odyssey. This is our earliest Greek literature, but the Greek language was already a highly developed language, proving that it had been in use long before this time.

2. Classical Greek: From about 600 B.C. on, some of the most magnificent literature that has ever been produced was written in Greek. This period sparkles with such names as Socrates, Plato, Aristotle, Thucydides, Herodotus, Xenophon, Sophocles, Euripides, and on and on. This is one of the brightest periods in the intellectual history of mankind.

3. *Koine* Greek: The fuller name for this is ἡ κοινὴ διάλεκτος, the common dialect. When Philip of Macedon and his son Alexander the Great made their great military conquests, they sought to spread the Greek language and culture as well. So successful were they that Greek became a universal language in the whole of the Mediterranean world. Most people, of course, knew it as a secondary language along with their own native language. It is not strange, then, that the *koine* Greek is a somewhat simpler language than Classical Greek. And we would expect to see certain reflections of a person's native language as he uses his secondary language, Greek.

We may date the *koine* period from about 333 B.C., the date of the battle of Issus, to about 330 A.D., when the seat of government was changed from Rome to Constantinople.

We have many papyri to illustrate this period. The Septuagint (LXX), the Greek translation of the Old Testament, is an early example of it. The slave-philosopher, Epictetus, the Greek church fathers, and others likewise use the Greek of this period. Of course, the New Testament is the most important part of the *koine* period.

4. Later Periods of the Greek Language: It is usually

129

customary to divide the rest of the Greek language into the Byzantine, or Mediaeval, down to 1453, the date of the fall of Constantinople, or the beginning of the Renaissance; and Modern Greek, from 1453 to the present.

Thus we can see that Greek has been a living language for more than three thousand years. As we study the New Testament we must remember that it is specifically *koine* Greek, but we can get a certain amount of help from a historical study of the language as a whole, particularly from the Classical period that immediately preceded it. We can get some help from a study of other languages that come from the same Indo-European group, particularly from the rather closely related Sanskrit and Latin. The more detailed work in the fields of historical and comparative grammar must be carried on by the highly trained experts in these fields.

Koine Compared with Classical Greek

Many students come to the New Testament from Classical Greek, so it may be helpful to note some of the differences between the two.

In general, there was a tendency toward greater simplicity and regularity. People who used Greek as a secondary language especially could not be expected to know and use all of the intricacies of the very complex Classical Greek.

The dual number, which was dying out in the Classical period, does not occur at all in the *koine* period. The singular and the plural numbers were considered sufficient.

The optative mood is dying away in the *koine* period, but it is still used. The student cannot completely ignore it.

Certain of the older, more irregular -μι verbs are developing -ω verb forms. From the verb ἵστημι, for example, come such verbs as στήκω, ἱστάνω, and ἱστάω. The stem δεικνυ- may have either μι or ω as its ending. This is a step in the right direction, but, unfortunately, it has not been carried far enough to eliminate the necessity of knowing the -μι verbs with all their difficulties.

130

The negative μή is taking over many of the usages of οὐ. The very complex Classical rules for the negatives may be replaced by the simple *koine* rule: οὐ is the negative for the indicative mood; μή, for everything else. In questions, οὐ and μή are still used, as in the Classical period, to imply positive and negative answers respectively.

ἵνα clauses have been greatly extended in the *koine* period. They still normally take the subjunctive mood, but often they take the future indicative, or occasionally even the present indicative. They still regularly express purpose, but they are often used also for all kinds of "that" clauses.

These are the major differences, but there are quite a few smaller ones as well that the student will soon pick up. For example, the Classical γίγνομαι and γιγνώσκω are in *koine* γίνομαι and γινώσκω.

CHAPTER XVI

SEMITISMS IN THE NEW TESTAMENT

One of the old theories of the New Testament language was that it was more Aramaic than Greek, written by men who knew Aramic well but Greek poorly. Then Deissmann showed that the language of the New Testament was the common Greek of that period. At first it was denied that there were any Hebraisms in the New Testament; everything was good *koine* Greek. More careful study has shown that that position was somewhat too extreme.

Nearly all of the writers of the New Testament books were Jews. They all knew something of the Hebrew of the Old Testament, and their primary language was the closely related Aramaic. It is only natural that they allowed their Semitic language to color their use of Greek, their secondary language. When an English-speaking student writes Greek he tends to use a definite article in Greek where there was one in English. In like manner we see at times a reflection of a Semitic idiom in the Greek of the New Testament.

Some few Semitic scholars claim to see so much Semitic influence in the New Testament that they have developed theories of Semitic originals for certain books of the New Testament. Those theories have never won the approval of New Testament scholarship, however.

Those who know Hebrew or Aramaic or both may use their knowledge of these languages to good effect in understanding some of the fine points of New Testament idiom. It is highly probable that Jesus Himself normally spoke Aramaic to His Jewish audiences, so His sayings in the Greek gospels are translations.

We welcome whatever help the Semitic scholars can give, but the New Testament books themselves were all written in *koine* Greek by men who had a good, competent knowledge of Greek. Help from Semitic sources will be very minor at best. Greek is the language of the New Testament.

CHAPTER XVII

FIGURES OF SPEECH IN THE NEW TESTAMENT

In a brief grammar we need do little more than mention the fact that the New Testament, like nearly all literature, contains various figures of speech. Students who know English rhetoric will recognize all the common figures of speech and will have no difficulty handling them--simile, metaphor, hyperbole, aposiopesis, personification, parable, allegory, and so on. They may need some help in handling such forms as apocalyptic literature and some of the mechanical features of Semitic or Greek poetry, but this help may be found in the more detailed grammars or in the better commentaries.

It might be well to emphasize the importance of dealing fairly with the figurative language of the Bible. If something that was meant to be a figure of speech is taken as simple matter-of-fact prose, violence is done to the original intended meaning. At times it is very easy to recognize figurative language, but at times the best scholars are not able to reach agreement about certain passages, which then must remain uncertain in meaning. Handling figurative language is something of an art as well as a science.

INDEX